The Illusion of Us:

The Suppression and Evolution of Human Consciousness

Matthew LaCroix

Second Edition

DEDICATION

This book would not be possible without the dedication and hard work of many brave minds and Truth seekers who have risked it all to allow for this information to come to light. It is to them that the greatest appreciation should be given.

CONTENTS

ACKNOWLEDGMENTS

Just to name a few: Colleen Forsyth, Ann LaCroix, Justin Mills, Ethan Silin, Barbara Marciniak, David Icke, Graham Hancock, Randall Carlson, Robert Temple, Dr Steven Greer, Zecharia Sitchin, Michio Kaku, Michael Tellinger, Robert Bauval, William Cooper, Dr. John Brandenburg, Mario Picon, Marc Peterson, Elena Calligaris, Gerald Clark, and Mark Passio.

CHAPTER 1

WHAT IS CONSCIOUSNESS?

For centuries, the question of what consciousness is has been one of the greatest ponderings of the human mind. Most of society shies away from even bringing up this taboo subject through fear of mockery and ridicule. How many classes were taught in school that dealt with deep expansive thought and the origins of consciousness? The greatest lie that has ever been orchestrated is the illusion of what human beings really are and the Truth behind our divine consciousness. The Chinese philosopher Lao Tzu once said, "The key to growth is the introduction of higher dimensions of consciousness into our awareness." By seeking out the true origins of our consciousness, a person leads down the pathway towards understanding the very framework of the universe itself.

The great search for seeking the individual Truths to our identity lies within our conscious expansion. That is why such great lengths have been taken in order to keep it secret and hidden from us for thousands of years. There is an awakening of consciousness occurring within humanity that is spreading across all corners of the world. Just as the ancient Mayans predicted, society has reached a time when the veil of illusion binding our consciousness within the chains of its own awareness are finally beginning to crumble all around us.

The famed philosopher Socrates and his inspired pupil Plato became powerful voices of deciphering this illusion that has been perpetrated on humanity for centuries. They realized the importance of what Truth represents in our society and how false information has the ability to define our own conscious reality for us. Both Socrates and Plato understood the power behind words and that only by searching within one's self can the absolute Truths finally be revealed. They believed that most people are too easily misled by false information and that political leaders should be chosen according to their understanding of the absolute Truths of life, derived from the fundamentals of philosophy. The practice of philosophy is rooted in answering life's greatest questions, which can only be found through conscious expansion. The reason for this unique style of learning is that the Truths which govern everything in the universe will always stay constant and remain genuine for all of time.

Hidden deep inside our consciousness, those Truths are desperately waiting to be heard. So then we must ask the question, what is absolute Truth? Absolute Truth is that which cannot be refuted or disproved when viewed through the lens of a rational, objective mind. Plato firmly believed that absolute Truth was so fundamentally important that the word itself should be only written with a capitol "T". I only wish to continue on his great legacy he left behind. The fundamental secret behind always arriving at Truth is by viewing information strictly from the perspective of an objective observer. Once an individual begins this journey of discovering Truth, they will quickly recognize the clear pattern laid out for us to follow. Like a scavenger hunt for knowledge, each piece fits into a running timeline which chronicles the story of all existence in the universe and the integral connections they each have to one another.

The most appropriate place to start when traveling down this road of Truth is by explaining that every human being has a different level of consciousness. These various levels of conscious awareness directly translate into the ability for a person to comprehend complex concepts and the bigger picture at hand for non-linear thinking. That means that for some people, based on their unique development skills and capacity for learning, will simply never be able to understand what I am talking about. Those individuals are not less important or dumb but are simply a byproduct of the hostile environment to which our consciousness can advance itself. By becoming consciously aware, it means that the individual has made the intention known within themselves to follow a certain path in life. Instead of being distracted by that which derails our development, we can each consciously choose to forge a new path for ourselves. We are all given the choice of freedom whenever we want it, but no matter how much convincing information is hurtled at a person, it is the individual who must ultimately decide on their own expansion.

In tackling such a massive and almost impossible topic to measure and prove, I would like to start by emphasizing: please be objective in everything in your life. Don't believe these words just because they are written but instead contemplate on them and see if you find Truth in them yourself. The goal of this book is to expand your conscious awareness and introduce you to a secret knowing that has been hiding in plain sight all along. I do not pretend to have all the answers, but I feel very humbled to have the ability to comprehend many of the clues left behind for us and fit them together into a timeline for humanity.

My only intention with these words is to continue the ancient traditions passed down for the preservation of Truth. I seek to peel back the veil that has encased humanity in the very illusion of itself and expose the framework for the most incredible story ever told. But beyond the fact that this information should be known, is the stark realization that it actually *must* be known, for the time of ignorance is quickly running out for us.

I write this book as more of a deep conversation between friends, sitting around a flickering fire deep in the wilderness somewhere, void of all distractions. I have chosen a different kind of style and one that I hope flows better and does not distract or bore the individual by dragging out repetitive themes. With so much misinformation constantly poisoning us from all directions, it can be very difficult to figure out what is real and what is a distraction of the Truth. I hope you sift through my words and separate the beneficial pieces for yourself. This book's only goal is to expand your consciousness to a new possibility and maybe even a new reality. Come with me, through the power of words, on this journey of self-awareness and discovery of who we really are. By the time you reach the end of this book I promise that you will never look at reality and this world the same way again.

The mysteries around consciousness and the universe have been the greatest fascinations of my lifetime. As far back as I can remember the concepts always left my head in the clouds deep in thought, wondering if the very world around me was merely an illusion. I simply could not accept the sad and simple, unconnected narrative being provided. That deep connection to all living things could be heard and even felt in the haunting cry of a loon, or the buzzing of a bee pollinating the flowers around me. That interconnectedness and hidden purpose for all living things constantly spoke to me throughout my life through quiet whispers and subliminal thoughts. It wasn't until years later that I was finally able to fully hear it and understand what was being said all along. With all this knowledge and Truth inside, I have felt a deeply pressing need to tell this incredible story of us and share with as many people as possible.

Terrence McKenna elegantly wrote, "You are an explorer, and you represent our species, and the greatest good you can do is to bring back a new idea, because our world is endangered by the absence of good ideas. Our world is in crisis because of the absence of consciousness." Those words echo through the fabric of my being and speak to humanity's continuous struggle with its own realization. We are living during such a pivotal time for the future of the human species that our continued existence will be determined by our ability to expand our consciousness.

Growing up in a world where we are taught that being different is a flaw there is a great need to conform to others. This thought process represents a reality which is manufactured for humanity that greatly benefits a uniformed way of thinking. An excellent indicator to help explain the levels of consciousness that various different people can have is through their imagination potential. Imagination is what drives creativity and stimulates unique thought. The process of imagining allows the user to create a virtual world of their own and by doing so, assists in expanding the mind's potential. Those who find themselves constantly lost in imagination are often the very same ones who have a higher capacity for understanding alternative thinking. It is to these expansive thinkers that I speak to most. Albert Einstein once said, "The real sign of intelligence isn't knowledge, but imagination." Some of us know who we are already, but there are many others who are just waking up to the realization behind the expansiveness of their mind. It isn't until the individual fully embraces and understands their uniqueness that they can reach their highest potential as a human species.

The human brain and consciousness are what determines this reality for us. The way we view life, death, and every action we take is defined by how we view our reality. Every morning we wake to a vibrant reality of wavelengths and frequencies that make up this three-dimensional world. The human brain, containing billions of neuron connections, is receiving information through the retinas in the eyes which is then being projected by the brain. We all contain a unique human experience that is determined by all the decisions we have made in our life and the associations that are bound to them. That means that each person has a slightly different version of this reality. Because the very reality we live in can be so unique, there has been a long standing attempt to define it for us. By defining our collective reality to what suits the needs of that predetermined model for society, the result has caused humanity to become severed off from the important connections back to the planet. This has led to the collective hijacking of human consciousness where our minds have literally been stolen from us to exist in nothing more than an illusion of itself.

What is real? That question has driven many who seek it to the very edge of insanity. Without a solid framework to fall back on, some minds have found themselves in a complete free fall with no bottom in sight. Realizing the reality projected before them is nothing more than an illusion, it often leaves emptiness and anger in its wake unless a spiritual connection can be made. This transitional point of awareness must be followed up with an understanding of who we really are and how we define ourselves in this physical world. If certain steps are not followed in re-forming our perceptions of reality and self, the person can be left in a scattered state of extreme fear and confusion. These teachings are intended to gently guide your conscious expansion while also helping to ground you and connect to a higher purpose and design.

I want to strongly emphasize that this mental transition is one of the hardest accomplishments a person can do in their lifetime. Carl Jung speaks to these challenges when he says, "There is no coming to consciousness without pain. People will do anything, no matter how absurd, in order to avoid facing their own soul. One does not become enlightened by imagining figures of light, but by making the darkness conscious."

Our culture considers the most impressive accomplishments of humanity to be those of pure physical willpower and pride themselves in the conquering of the world's tallest peaks and deepest oceans. The Truth is, the greatest journey we can make is within our own mind, through conscious expansion. That is what ultimately drives the evolution of a species, beyond the simple domination of its resources. Without conscious expansion, a developing species will either destroy itself through war or be forced to leave their dying planet in search of other means of survival. I strive to connect the Truths of our history as well as reality and to avoid so much of the misinformation that constantly distracts us from every direction.

The way human beings discern reality is defined by how they perceive associated information in their brains, so we must understand that our minds can be controlled through the manipulation of that incoming information. When you begin to look at things from the outside as an observer, the very reality you thought was real turns out to be nothing more than a mirage of manipulation. What if the very perception of who we are and our true history was completely created to control us? Through the use of materialism, money, fear, and pre-defining our own existence, most of humanity walks around in an artificial illusion of reality. This illusion has taken over everything in our world. It is the illusion of what consciousness really is and our role in the universe. The way this is achieved is by making us believe consciousness is created by the brain and thus, that we are nothing more than an intelligent, evolved animal, struggling to survive here. This misconception is fueled through a state of constant war and the domination over remaining resources from our dying planet.

The hardest part of this perceptional learning to fully grasp, is how exactly reality has been stolen from us. This ancient heist of our consciousness that began thousands of years ago, has exponentially manifested into the current model of our slumbering reality. Imagine how you might feel from seeing a shimmering, snowcapped mountain in the distance, or a homeless man sleeping in a dirty alleyway. To some they see beauty and sadness, and others, maybe nothing really at all. That Truth governs how the world operates and what **becomes** reality. If a certain reality is determined to be more appropriate for large populations of people, that reality can be created out of laws, money, history, and society. Reality is defined for us only by what we are told is real by those in authoritative roles. All of our perceptions of that reality are based on what we learn in school and from society around us. But for those who have found themselves standing on a distant mountain, staring into the heavens and wondering if there isn't more to this life than what we have been told, these words will resonate within you and spark a feeling inside that has been there all along.

This control of reality and information is fed to the general population from within governments and the heads of mainstream religions. This is accomplished through the trickling down of misinformation, manipulated through the teaching of incorrect human history and understanding consciousness. Generation upon generation, the Truth, and connection to this planet have been slowly eroded from us and nearly lost to time. All of our egotistical accomplishments have forced a false sense of entitlement over the Earth. Before long, the majority of people simply do not see beauty any longer and to them, it is just a background while they move to their next destination. Pulled down by the weight of this emptiness, our childlike wonder of the world, like the light of a candle, barely flickers any longer and threatens to go out.

There are many who have shattered this perception and are no longer bound by its restraint. Like finding a hole in the fence, these individuals have broken out of the enclosure and run away from the herd to find themselves in a place where their consciousness is no longer confined by control and manipulation. Far away from the sickness that corrupts our mind, the true reality of this world awaits us, hidden beneath layers of our own ego. Peeling back these layers reveals a spectacular world around us, where our every action is intricately connected to our own development and feeds into the incredible running narrative of the entire universe. Brian Cox said, "We are the cosmos made conscious and life is the means by which the universe understands itself." In the end, we must ask ourselves, what part did we play in this story?

This information can be quite startling for many and even scary, but the Truth is there is nothing to fear. Fear is a leftover remnant of the ancient left brain and is not actually real. We manifest fear based on the stimuli around us and let it determine our thoughts. When we are able to confront and conquer our greatest fears we will truly be free. Later on in the book, you will read about how fear has been used as the ultimate weapon against conscious expansion. Humans dominated by fear will revert back to their primitive survival state since they feel their life is in jeopardy. The conscious evolution of our species has been held hostage by this model of control through fear. Humanity is tormented by its past and allows it to dictate its very future. It is only when we see that fear is merely just an illusion that we will be finally free and move beyond its hold over us.

We must question everything in our reality and wake up the atrocities that have been perpetrated on our society. There is a desperate race to learn this Truth before our species annihilates our self through this derived confusion. Once one breaks free of this illusion, they find a hidden world exists full of light and humbling amazement. Modern society rarely even considers the fact that we are on a planet flying through space, with billions of other suns and galaxies in an almost infinitely expansive universe. Even the stars have become simply backdrop to people, who rarely look up at them any longer as they pass by underneath.

We have become a society that worships celebrities and makes fun of high intelligence. Everything is geared towards keeping us in a small box of thinking. Meanwhile, we are left with an empty world, slaving for money and following an oligarchy system of control. It makes me cry when I think about what has happened to human beings as I try and comprehend all of the stolen lives that have never really lived. I see the potential of what is and what has happened in striking contrast to one another. Through understanding what consciousness really is, it becomes a powerful tool and means of waking up.

Let me take you down a far different path, to a highly guarded place I like to call the real reality. They call this thinking traveling down the rabbit hole because once you get a glimpse of the Truth you yearn for more and it expands your world deeper than you ever thought possible. The most difficult step to take in this discovery of the Truth really is the first one. Staring into the abyss of information that challenges the very paradigm of our reality can be very difficult and uncomfortable to undertake. The ability to break free of all of the lies and deceit that has been perpetrated on humanity revolves around the individual's reliability on the system itself. The more they are dependent on it for happiness and stability, the more difficult it will be to let go. Once you do finally take that difficult first step and begin to piece together the incredible story of now, it becomes very difficult to go back to your previous mindset because your subconscious already knows the Truth. Through learning and expanding conscious awareness to new information and the world around us, the ability to comprehend complex ideas increases dramatically. That is why so many people who have a lack of information simply cannot comprehend or understand this.

The human brain is capable of storing and understanding tremendous amounts of information. Our organic bodies are housing the most complex thing we know of in the universe. Human beings only use about 10% of their brain capacity at one time showing the true potential of what lies ahead for our evolution. If we were to contrast the brain size and complexity from our past ape ancestors to that of modern Homo sapiens, the comparison of neurological activity wouldn't even be remotely similar. That simple view is precisely how our mindset has been locked in a dark cave of its own Darwinism, by perceiving our very identity as nothing more than an evolved ape. The idea that the human brain simply doubled its size over a very short period of time due to simple evolution is illogical when looking at all the evidence. We must separate ourselves out from this primitive viewpoint in order to fully see the Truth in our identity.

This incredible gift of consciousness endowed within humanity, allows our unique ability to perceive everything in the universe, as well as where we fit in ourselves. Without a manual to come with this incredibly powerful organic computer, we simply flail about, being influenced by anything shiny that entices our thirst for pleasure. On this path of consciousness evolution, we must first answer the question that has held us back for so long. What is reality? We are here together to try and shed light on that very question. Society heavily promotes the premise that the physical world is the great feat to conquer in this life, yet it is the journey through self that has the greatest rewards. We have been steered away from emotion, because though emotion we can connect to our highest state of consciousness and discover ultimate Truth. That severed connection is what denies our very expansion.

Now you can imagine this disassociation with reality may cause society to act a certain way. If the burger flipper realizes he is actually his own multidimensional consciousness that resides in the astral plane, he may choose different career choices. Simply thinking about consciousness existing outside of your brain is expansion in itself. That is where I want you to wander to and dip a toe into the waters of our divine connection to all of life itself. Human consciousness exists on a multidimensional sphere, simply being housed in this organic body. We are merely receivers of information, residing in this three-dimensional, physical world, constantly searching for the right path to take in our story. Only through experience are we able to decide for ourselves what is real and what is a suppression of consciousness.

As crazy as this information may sound to some think for a moment about the five senses we regularly use. If we were to try and perceive something outside of those five senses, we simply would be unable to even know it was there. The same principle is true for dimensions. We know of a three-dimensional world because that is all we can see. It is the world around us that we ever increasingly take for granted. Understand that right now quantum physics dictates there are likely more than ten different dimensions. Try and think about that for a moment and let it sink in. Very quickly you realize that we live in a small mind set world, which revolves around fighting over frivolous material things as nothing more than a clever distraction from the Truth.

When I emphasize that consciousness exists on another dimensional plane, it must be viewed as the true identity of the individual, not the physical body. That is the great Illusion of Us and the vice that holds us firmly in this false perception. You must see consciousness as an incredible gift and the most humbling of experiences. That connection to the higher self has been severed through the manipulation of our identity and thus, forming an artificial reality. Human beings hold the ability to unlock our true potential through conscious expansion and the secrets within our DNA. That is the reason that our awakening to this Truth has been fought over and guarded for so long from us.

All of our history of hopes, dreams, ideas, inventions and even deepest love all come from conscious expansion. It is what carries us forward and drives us to be better. Only through the duality of learning is this possible which is what binds all of this together. You must experience the good and the bad and then choose who you identify with and follow that path inside you. That path can either lead you to enlightenment and connection, or illusion and sadness. This isn't a religious choice or some New Age cult following, but the essential decision we must make within ourselves. But most importantly to appreciate the good you must first know the bad. The more you look the more you see everything is governed by this teaching duality world. That is how we define our true identity through consciousness, grown through the experiences and learning we get to have in this beautiful place called Earth.

All of these interwoven and connected experiences contribute to the entire narrative that is our story of humanity. Written in the pages of time we forge our future based on our past and hopefully learn from those mistakes. Driven by confusion, greed, lust, and ego, we dominate and destroy the only home we have ever known. With the fear of death always ruling our decisions, we squander away everything and care little about the future or the consequences of our actions. Very quickly you begin to see that the illusion of humanity is merely a tool for controlling our consciousness. Once the veil of darkened Truth is lifted, all that remains is indescribable beauty and connectedness to all things. In order to exist there, our minds need some training first to break free of the prison that binds it.

Continue on this story with me as we explore consciousness further and dive into the incredible history of humanity. I know that so many of these words speak to something deep down inside of us, hidden away, until the right time that it can be heard. This book is for all of those inquisitive minds who have a quench for

Truth and knowledge and simply do not accept the represented reality around them. Deeper and deeper we will travel, following the breadcrumbs of Truth, until we can finally understand the greatest story ever told. (1, 3)

CHAPTER 2

OUR HIDDEN HISTORY

If you are still reading this, it means you are willing to think outside the tightly controlled perspective given for human history that has been manipulated for thousands of years. From the great pyramids of Giza to the Mayan temples of Mexico, our species has a fascinating history that predates us, showing the important connections humanity once had to the natural world and to the universe itself. These ancient monuments, pyramids, and forgotten cities hold the keys to finding out the Truth about our past. From the illogical and unscientific theories given to the public for how these structures were constructed and the linear narratives portrayed, the Truth behind our lost history is just starting to emerge now. The most important gift you can give a developing species is not a material thing but knowledge itself. Knowledge can lead to infinite possibilities and outcomes for the future.

So much of human history has been kept secret from us and heavily guarded. If we were to know the Truth it would change the very idea of how we perceive ourselves and reality itself. If this information and disclosure came out too fast, there would be global anarchy and violence as so many would realize their life is a lie. The Truth is so incredible that only an expansive mind can even comprehend its overall size and scope. Realize that as you are reading this, a critically important struggle is playing out all around us over the right to free will within a conscious species. Most of us are simply unaware of any of it happening.

Try to fully comprehend the idea of existing on a planet in the far outer edges of the Milky Way Galaxy. The Milky Way is one of the trillions of other galaxies in the universe which would outnumber every grain of sand on planet Earth. Allow that staggering number and sheer size and scale sink in. Reality will start to blur and soon you become an observer in this galactic adventure, aware of yourself. This mindset is essential for understanding the great complexity to our universe. Never underestimate the potential of what is possible in this grand theater of experience and the evolution of consciousness.

There is a very tight narrative used to show a steady progression of evolution from apes to humans. It all seems very basic and gives the illusion of randomness to all life. It is truly sad to think about how many people's lives have been ruined and made into a literal hell by not understanding the Truths behind our incredible identity. Yet society believes wholeheartedly everything they have been told and is cleverly trained to attack any new ideas that challenge the status quo. We must throw away much of what we think we know and start from scratch. In telling the story of humanity, understand that some of this information is still somewhat unknown from thousands of years of suppression and destruction and represents a narrative carefully laid out from extensive research. This is by no means the entire story of humanity, for it would take volumes and almost infinite sources to complete.

Long before human beings lived on Earth, the planet was ruled by the dinosaurs. Understanding that giant lizards ruled the Earth for 200 million years is important for the context of where we fit in. If we did not have the overwhelming evidence left behind for their existence, dinosaurs would have just as likely have ended up as nothing more than myth and legend. One cannot help but draw parallels back to this comparison for how society relates to our historical events. Even the farthest drawn out timeline for humanity would be but a tiny echo in the total history of species living here on planet Earth. People casually think of dinosaurs as all extinct, yet all around us they are present. From birds to crocodiles, they have been here all along. It is only the illusion of progression that has changed our perception. People must remember who was here first when pretending we are mighty owners of this planet. We must not think of dinosaurs as just the ancient bones from the past, but rather, as the missing link in understanding our very future.

The only way we can piece together the past is from the clues we have and our ability to connect them correctly. The teachings and writings that align with our promoted history are taught to the population in order to generate a timeline that is used to dictate how we perceive ourselves. That narrative has been artificially created to falsely hide the Truth. Our mainstream religions have been re-written and the majority of history as we know it is largely fabricated and greatly altered. This incredibly clever collective hijacking of history, religion, education, and monetary systems has formed the matrix of illusion that has become our reality. We commonly think of virtual reality as just an electronic device, but we ourselves are simply organic computers that have been programmed to serve a form of conscious slavery. By keeping people asleep of our past, our future has been temporarily stolen from us.

So now let us clear the board and wipe clean our preconceptions of everything. Our education system follows a strictly regulated curriculum, where generations of people have been coerced into learning one version of history, reinforced through books and propaganda shown on television. This artificially created perception of history, along with the illusion of our purpose and existence, has led to the control of our reality.

Consider for a moment the Fuente Magna Bowl which was found in 1958 by a farmer in Bolivia and has been carbon dated to over 5000 years old. What makes the bowl so unusual are the inscriptions found inside which match precisely with Sumerian cuneiform writings from the ancient Mesopotamian area of Iraq. Both of these civilizations are portrayed in our history books as somewhat primitive and utilizing nothing more than simple hand tools. So how is it then that these isolated cultures, which were separated by thousands of miles of ocean, somehow managed to develop the same complex writing style? Perhaps a more prudent question is why has no one ever heard of this evidence?

Humanity's entire history on Earth is but a tiny blip in the overall timeline of life on the planet and we must separate ourselves from thinking we represent a significant part of its past. Our awareness is limited by only what we are told is true and most of us never consider questioning that principle. I instead take you down a very different version with the aid of a lot of brave archaeologists and thinkers, who are willing to take on the entire establishment controlling history. If you have the courage to dig deep enough and the insight and vision to comprehend how the complex puzzle fits together, a transcendent connection of knowing falls over the enlightened thinker. It's as if the Truth desperately wanted to be known and was waiting to be heard all along. Come with me down the updated history of humanity and the incredible secrets that have been heavily guarded against ever being known. You will never see reality the same way again.

The first and most necessary place to start is by understanding the universe around us. This is essential in order to become an objective observer of history. The galaxy we live in, called the Milky Way, contains billions of other Earth-like planets and suns, some of which are over a hundred times larger than ours. When we step outside to observe the seemingly endless night sky sparkling above us, what we perceive as the entire universe is merely a tiny window of the outer fringes of our galaxy. This minuscule glimpse of awareness represents only a small fraction of the vast complexities found within the universe. The nearest galaxy to ours, known as the Andromeda galaxy, is 2.5 million light years away. To put that in perspective, if we had the capability to travel at the speed of light, it would take us 2.5 million years to arrive there. That incredibly long distance is an essential aspect of the cosmic hierarchy system of conscious evolution.

If an intelligent species develops the capability to travel these tremendous distances, then it would have to fully understand the intricate properties of how the universe itself worked. These insurmountable and almost mind-boggling distances between even neighboring suns would allow only those of far superior knowledge, living within an advanced society to reach them. Consider the fact that there are more than a trillion planets within our galaxy alone which are able to support developing life. If an interstellar civilization was able to travel to one of these planets they could alter the entire future of that species. This fundamental principle is very similar to what happens when modern technology finds its way to a remote tribe hidden in the jungle. These developing species are extremely vulnerable to outside influences and even simple contact can drastically alter their future. The vast distances between planets and suns is necessary in order to allow the unaltered development of the native species. Great caution must be taken from any advanced civilization that travels to one of these planets since their influences could critically alter the delicate development stage for those living there. All of this information must be considered to fully comprehend the story of humanity.

In the early 1930's, two French anthropologists visited a remote tribe called the Dogon people in Mali, Africa. The Dogon tribe had extensive and advanced knowledge of celestial star systems, with a heavy emphasis on the constellation of Canis Major and the Dog Star known as Sirius. They knew of precise details for the elliptical orbits of the suns of Sirius A, B, and even a tiny third sun called C. The unknown question at the time and the important link for proving an intelligent outside influence, lies in the fact that Sirius B cannot be seen by the naked eye and wasn't photographed until 1970 by radio telescope. Yet somehow this knowledge had been well known and passed down for hundreds of generations. Even more impressive is that the Dogon people speak of a third star, called Sirius C, that hasn't even been discovered yet by modern astronomy.

This seemingly simple and primitive tribe in western Africa somehow possessed and understood vast amounts of information about our galaxy that modern science is just catching up with discovering today. The Dogon people have retained their heritage and ancient knowledge they say was given to them by great beings known as the Nommo and passed down this vital information for thousands of years. The most logical question we must ask ourselves is who are the Nommo?

With only a select few elders chosen to hold this knowledge, they dedicate their life to its protection and lock themselves away from the world in order to protect its purity. The Dogon people went to these great lengths because they knew how important this information was and passed down this knowledge from generation to generation in isolation. In retracing the Dogon people's heritage, it can be fascinating to find out that they were originally from Egypt and escaped to Mali in order to avoid religious persecution. So now let us now go back, as we retrace the steps taken by the Dogon people that lead us back to ancient Egypt, where many of the answers to humanity can be found buried beneath the sands of time. All of these important contributions form stepping stones that bridge an important gap and allow for us to understand our true history. Without all of these sacrifices, humanity might have remained in the dark forever.

Arriving in ancient Egypt, we find a wealth of evidence all pointing towards the extraterrestrial influences that shaped the past and represent a portal into understanding the roots of our ancestors. The great pyramids of the Giza Plateau, if viewed from the air, are all aligned geometrically perfect to the three stars that make up the belt of the Orion Constellation. Inside the largest of the Giza pyramids, there are vertical shafts that point directly to Orion's Belt and Sirius. Both of these constellations have a rich history with Egypt, Mexico, Peru, and much of the Middle East, into southern Asia. All of these cultures sculpted similar artifacts and inscriptions portraying these beings and their various craft used to travel here. Distinct links can be found in the progression of these ancient human civilizations advancing and also the designing of relics showing these 'gods' who influenced them. This forgotten relationship and the entire history of where we came has been heavily suppressed from the public. The monuments that still remain on the surface are seen as simply interesting background to most as they casually pass by to snap a few photos.

In 1945, one of the most important archaeological discoveries in all of history was made in central Egypt, near the Nile River. It was during the height of World War II and the discovery largely remained unknown from the general knowledge. To this day few have ever even heard of the Nag Hammadi Library. In our society, the greatest archaeological discoveries are portrayed to us as containing numerous valuable items and unimaginable wealth. That view is simply part of the illusion for what is really important. The Nag Hammadi Library contained the greatest gift of all, knowledge. Other great libraries, such as the library of Alexandria, have been totally lost to us from destruction and fire. With the devastating loss of these great libraries so too went much of human history and all of the great teachings from those who echoed before us.

The fundamentally important piece of this puzzle to understand is that the loss of these great libraries in our history was deliberate and orchestrated. If the knowledge that describes our past could be destroyed and re-written, then the future can be controlled. The Nag Hammadi Library was deliberately buried and sealed off like a time capsule, only to be opened for a time when humanity could hopefully find the information under freedom and without being prosecuted. Knowing that the connection to this Truth and our history was being systematically destroyed and wiped out, the Gnostics had no choice but to bury it. If not for this discovery, we never would have had so many important pieces of the puzzle.

This important library was created by the ancient Gnostic people from the teachings of the being known as Enoch. The Nag Hammadi Scriptures represented a collaboration of knowledge which follows the same principles from the Creator of All and are known as the Hermetic writings. The name "Hermetic" comes from the name Hermes; which is connected back to a being known as Thoth or Ningishzida in ancient Sumer. Other Hermetic writings such as the Emerald Tablets echo much of the same knowledge portrayed by Enoch and the Gnostics, yet they were found halfway across the world, sealed under a pyramid in Teotihuacan, Mexico. The Nag Hammadi Scriptures formed the original base for most of the religions of the world. The real question is who was Enoch and was he connected somehow to Hermes and Quetzalcoatl?

Much of Gnostic's work was re-written and heavily edited to create versions of religious text that seek to block off knowledge of the Truth of our past and the important chakra centers of the body that lead to conscious expansion. Religion was originally based on the important teachings that provided assistance for reaching the spiritual side of our nature but was later hijacked during the collapse of the Roman Empire by Constantine 1st, along with other powerful rulers and gods who turned it into the ultimate form of control. The famous symbol of the sacrifice on the cross represents the infiltration and corruption by the jealous god Marduk, also known as Amun-Ra who stole the teachings of his brother Thoth and pretended he was the savior of humanity while he extended his reign on Earth. This worship of Amun-Ra is still being practiced today whenever a person invokes the words Amen while praying.

The Nag Hammadi Scriptures and other Hermetic writings bridge a gap in understanding of so much of our history and identity. They speak about a false illusion that has been created here which creates a veil over our perceptions and awareness. The Emerald Tablets and Gnostic writings explain in detail about who we really are as divine light beings who are simply blocked off from knowing our true potential and connections back to the Creator of All. The answers to our history and who we are can be found by understanding these Hermetic writings and relating them directly to modern string theory. Only through the collaboration of these great teachings with quantum science can the full picture finally begin to show itself.

There are countless other writings, sculptures, and pyramids, scattered across the ancient world that make up the fragments which all lead to the bigger story. Scattered beneath dense jungles and towering above searing deserts, many of these ancient cultures knew they had to protect the Truth somehow so that it would survive to see the light of a new time. The greatest story ever told had to be protected for those brave adventurers and thinkers of the future, willing to challenge it all in the name of furthering humanity. In reading this timeline, understand that I do not wish to mislead or confuse, but only to connect with what has already been lost to us. Before we travel further down the rabbit hole, I want to leave with you a famous quote by Sir Arthur Conan Doyle, which is meant to be a reassuring voice of reason, when all seems lost. "Once you eliminate the impossible, whatever remains, no matter how improbable, must be the Truth." Let those words guide you as you decide your own version of reality.

In order to arrive at Truth, we must first cast out the deeply seeded pessimist inside of our ego and objectively consider the information I present. I do not simply throw random ideas together or create a false narrative which isn't directly based on a wealth of connected breadcrumbs of information. In figuring out the true story of us, I was constantly in a state of amazement and awe in learning about this story. Countless times I simply could not believe or accept the ideas I was coming across and I don't expect you to right away either. It wasn't until I understood the entire picture, through the uncovering of mountains of evidence to prove it to myself. I had to return to ideas over and over to build a foundation of knowledge in order to finally have that moment of understanding which is necessary. I can assure you though, I would not write anything here that I did not believe was Truth. We should embrace the incredible history preceding us and not let ego ever rule our judgment. There are always two sides of a story and I hold no grievances against any of those who came here.

We must move past the idea that we are alone in the galaxy, let alone the universe. There are millions of habitable planets with intelligent life, scattered in the billions of solar systems surrounding suns that allow habitable climates. Think of suns as enormous mothers, giving life to their small planets revolving around them, pulled in by their giant gravitational radius. New suns are born that create entirely new solar systems of their own and then they eventually die. It is a delicate balance of birth and rebirth that replays itself out over and over in the universe. Understand that the entire universe is a connected living organism, spreading its branches out like a tree and supporting the continued evolution of its own awareness through human consciousness.

There has been a monumental history predating us that we only have bits and pieces for what occurred. With an almost complete suppression of information, except for the scraps which have been lucky enough to remain, this history of humanity is a timeline based on all the evidence we have, built on the backs of the brave minds and researchers that preceded me. Without their courage and sacrifice, none of this would be possible. Remember, history is always written by the victors and that very fact clouds its purity. Put aside all predetermined ideas of what we have been told is our story and try and contemplate this for a moment.

Envision a timeline of advanced intelligent life, spanning millions of years in parts of our galaxy and multitudes of others. If you were to place where human beings fit in it would be but a minuscule blip in this record of time. Just think of all that has happened in the universe before humanity even existed. Now imagine if a planet, so incredibly special and unique that it was worth traveling across the cosmos to reach was being fought over for control. You will have to decide for yourself what is real in life and what is simply just a distraction of the Truth.

Let me take you on a journey down an alternate timeline for Earth and one that may resonate deep inside you, awakening a spark of wonder. In 1849 a spectacular discovery was made by Austen Henry Layard in Mosul, Iraq where seven clay tablets were found known as the Enuma Elish. The tablets contained symbols etched in stone, known as cuneiform writings, which pre-date nearly all other known historical records and gives a rare glimpse into the unaltered records of the past. The tablets tell the creation story of Earth out of the bowels of a planet called Tiamat and a great battle in the heavens by these Anunnaki gods.

According to the ancient writings, far in our distant past a smaller invader solar system became trapped within our central sun and led to disastrous collisions and turmoil during each perihelion pass. The planet Tiamat was struck by an unknown planet or moon and led to the eventual formation of Earth and the asteroid belt, known to these ancients as the Hammered Bracelet.

After the Earth cooled enough to support life it became seeded with prokaryotic organisms and later eukaryotes from advanced civilizations who saw a great vision and plan for the planet. The process of complex life appearing seems to follow a timeline for the evolution of the planet and not of the macro evolution of the species residing there. What that means is that as a planet's climate become more favorable and less hostile, it becomes a candidate for more advanced life being brought there. The physical change of a species over time, based on its unique environment is known as micro evolution. We must throw out the incorrect and antiquated model of evolution presented by Darwin to forge a new understanding for how complex life begins.

Consider the fact that Earth is a part of a vast number of habitable planets in our Milky Way Galaxy and beyond that contain rich amounts of life. As advanced cultures all over the universe developed the capabilities of interplanetary travel, there was a need to design a place where species and information could be stored safely. These planets, with optimal climates and environments, supported countless numbers of species. The Earth was considered one of the most unique planets in the galaxy and visited by countless advanced civilizations. It was where the plan first started and was the hallmark of what was later known as the living library on Earth.

The living library on Earth was a collaboration of plant and animal DNA brought here from all over the cosmos by advanced senescent civilizations. The Earth was designed as a free will zone where important genetics could be contributed and protected. Careful planning was done alongside the pre-existing species on the planet to create a spectacular living library of life that filled every corner of this world. This collaboration exceeded all expectations and the living library became a jewel of shimmering light in our solar system.

The Earth was chosen for the developing human species to evolve under the watchful eyes of these ancient guardians. Humanity was an experiment in housing frequency and unique DNA within a special humanoid body. Everything was going according to plan until certain beings came here and decided they wanted some of the resources that the colony of Earth provided. Because this planet is in a free will zone no one was allowed to own it. Planets similar to Earth exist all over the universe in various stages of their own evolutionary development.

Around 450,000 years ago, a group of advanced beings known as the Anunnaki traveled to the Earth from an unknown planet. They came here for specific resources and greatly disrupted the timeline of Homo sapiens. We know of this arrival period and history from numerous ancient texts, primarily from the ancient Sumerian people who wrote the Enuma Elish, which goes into extensive detail about their past influences on Earth.

Nearly all information surrounding the existence and location of a mysterious planet in the outer reaches of our solar system has been carefully guarded by NASA and other agencies. The Truth about Planet X has been heavily suppressed and confused with the term Nibiru, which actually references Jupiter. Robert Harrington, the head astronomer at the United States Naval Observatory became focused on finding the mysterious Planet X after observing gravitational disruptions in the orbits of Neptune and Uranus. Upon observing the planet on the IRAS probe in 1983, Harrington traveled to the southern tip of New Zealand where it is believed he observed the incoming planet on an 8-inch telescope in 1993. Shortly after this discovery, Robert Harrington was found dead of cancer and all of his work was immediately debunked as simply mathematical error. The Truth behind this planet represents one of the greatest secrets kept from humanity of all time.

The arrival and influence from these various advanced cultures on Earth does not follow a simple linear narrative or understanding. The complex timeline for the history of this planet represents countless cultures that have been on and off Earth for millions of years. Due to Earth's relative location in the Milky Way Galaxy and the overabundance of life and rare elements, this planet has always been intrinsically important to countless senescent civilizations who traveled here. There is overwhelming evidence to support this information for those who are brave enough to challenge the tightly controlled view given for the past. The Truth behind our history can be found from within the great pyramids of Giza, to the ancient monolithic cities buried beneath jungles and hundreds of feet of seawater. In all of these ancient human cultures, sometimes separated by thousands of miles of ocean, archaeologists have discovered countless, nearly identical statues and monuments all depicting various gods who traveled to Earth. The time for debate over the existence of intelligent extraterrestrial life is over. We must now look towards the influences they have had on past human civilizations in order to find evidence for the real story.

Ancient sites like that of Gobekli Tepe in Turkey, prove without a doubt the existence of advanced human cultures thousands of years before our current history books are willing to admit. Furthermore, in the timeline we are taught in school, human beings who were living more than 10,000 years ago were portrayed as slowly evolving and still considered hunters and gatherers. This conclusion is not based on a collaboration of all evidence in an unbiased manner, but rather deliberately selected evidence, which funnels into a predetermined narrative. The air needs to be cleared from the status of this information as this is no longer pseudoscience. If these cultures had advanced tools and technologies long before we are told they possessed them, then it should be realized that they received this knowledge from beyond our planet. When searching for Truth, the answer is almost always the result of what fits together in a sequence, regardless of where that path leads.

The Nag Hammadi Library and the Book of Enoch give us a rare glimpse into the un-altered writings of what the Bible would have contained. These lost texts give us a far more complete understanding of who the 'gods' were and their purpose here. The Book of Enoch talks extensively about visitors called the 'Watchers' who resided on Earth and never left. The ancient Sumerian people refer to these visitors as the Anunnaki, which means "those who from heaven to Earth came." All of these ancient writings and tablets paint us a clear picture of who these gods really were and to separate out what has become simply a myth to the human species. Even in the modern book of Genesis, a giant hybrid race of humans known as the Nephilim is mentioned, yet few even question its meaning or who they were. All of this ancient information paints a story for the past events on Earth and who was here.

Throughout the Bible, these beings, with far advanced technology, are always considered god(s) and thought of as divine. Yet, this wording would imply that there are multiple gods that somehow control the Earth, and instead of questioning this logic, humans have openly accepted it as just religious stories. All throughout history, stories have been told and carried down through generations, mentioning these gods frequently. These elaborate stories have become nothing more than mythology to the modern human race. Many of these tales are represented as exaggerated metaphors and taken at simple face value. However, there is almost always an element of Truth in them as well. People think of dragons, wizards, and giants, as nothing more than a laughable fairy tale, even though these depictions have turned up in stories and drawings all over the world. Many of the older Asian cultures, like the Japanese, have worshiped the dragon from their earliest records and have placed it on their official flags and banners to commemorate them. Despite all of these commonly used motifs cropping up virtually everywhere today, the vast majority of people still just see them as nothing more than fantasy.

The 'gods' that came here were more than a million years ahead of human evolution and possess such advanced knowledge and technology that they can exist in higher dimensions that humans cannot even perceive. These beings have the ability to become physical here but can instead choose to stay in higher realms and force others to do their bidding. Similar to our sensory perception of a radio wave, since it is outside our dimensional awareness it is invisible to us. The visitors used advanced technology to keep Earth in a specific vibrational frequency, allowing for the total manipulation of reality within the developing human species. That is how the human farm was able to ultimately remain hidden from the collective of our awareness. We understand so little about the universe in our small three-dimensional world and yet our naivety causes us to be blinded from all Truth through stubborn ignorance. With quantum physics dictating well over ten dimensions, the time for expanding our perceptional possibilities is long overdue. Humanity's view of reality is built upon the polluted associations from the past and this leads to the illusion for how we define it now.

For hundreds of thousands of years, there has been an ancient dispute over the right to free will within a consciously developing species. The hierarchical system of evolution in the cosmos for intelligent beings governs nearly all decisions for those species that exist in dimensions below them. The rights to the ownership of Earth and disrupting its important timeline led to disputes for control of the planet and its resources. Earth and its living library was considered extremely valuable and important to many of the senescent civilizations who helped design it. One side cared deeply for the future of this library and the freedoms of the human species, while the other for control of resources and domination of the planet. That is why the concept of light battling against darkness is used throughout our culture. Light is always associated with the freedom of information and spiritual growth, while darkness is associated with the suppression of consciousness through domination. These visitors conquered light and the Earth became a place of darkness under their control for hundreds of thousands of years. Humanity is now finally beginning to emerge out of this darkness that has consumed so much of our true identity and awareness.

Some of the evidence that exists for past conflicts in our solar system can still be seen on some of the planets and moons around Earth. Mars is an example of the fallout of one of these devastating wars which occurred long before humanity on Earth even existed. The Martian atmosphere was obliterated from nuclear weapons and an entire planet turned into a radioactive wasteland. Strong indicators for this hypothesis come from probe analysis that was done of the planet's atmosphere, which has shown abnormally high amounts of Uranium and Thorium, elements which are present together only after a nuclear explosion. Further evidence can be seen with the red coloring of the surface soil, largely due to immense amounts of radioactive isotopes covering the entire planet. The aftermath of these explosions on Mars resulted in the loss of nearly all of the water on the planet, which quickly evaporated into space, leading to almost all life ceasing to exist there.

Imagine a planet, once rich with life, with large oceans and advanced cultures, now existing as nothing more than an echo of the past. That is the horror that can occur on a planet from nuclear annihilation. Remnants of ancient civilizations have been seen and mostly covered up. If we want to look at what an apocalyptic, alternate future for Earth could be, we simply look at Mars. Take a moment to gain a little perspective on our current situation on Earth and the many similarities that come up between the two timelines. Will the human race, with all of its ego and domination for natural resources, lead to its own mutual destruction and become nothing more than a lost memory like Mars? That future is dangling on the edge of our own slumbering awareness.

There have been many names used throughout history to describe the advanced extraterrestrial species that have been on and off this planet for thousands of years. Their names have been found in countless ancient writings and recorded as the Pleiadians, Archons, Anunnaki, Djinn, Draconians, Nommo, Reptilians, Igigi, or even the Watchers, but the Anunnaki civilization is most relevant to our history. All the way back to our earliest scriptures and writings we have seen evidence of these names mentioned repeatedly from cultures in Japan and Egypt, all the way to Mexico and Peru. These cultures were separated by thousands of miles of ocean and yet they carved statues and figures that were all of a similar extra-terrestrial appearance, which commonly represented that of a very tall being with an elongated skull. The gods of history must be realized for what they really were and not worshiped as some higher deity we must simply obey. Countless connections can be traced back to the ancient world, showing the intrinsic contributions that these visitors made to human societies all over the planet. These sudden advancements were only possible because of the visitor's unique knowledge of the universe and monolithic building techniques. The Anunnaki should be known as the great master builders of the past and are responsible for the largest structures on Earth such as the pyramids of Giza. This information cannot be brushed off as a simple coincidence and instead should be seen as tangible evidence for their direct influence on developing human cultures all throughout history.

The most compelling evidence that has remained to show who the Anunnaki really were can be found in ancient Babylonian and Sumerian cuneiform tablets such as the Enuma Elish, Epic of Gilgamesh, or the Atrahasis which are only now being fully understood and accepted. These clues to the past completely re-write the given narrative for our entire history and even religion. What these tablets describe to us is the Truth behind our creation story along with understanding who these advanced beings really were and how they have shaped our society.

The Anunnaki traveled to Earth primarily for the rare element Au, or gold because of its incredibly important properties. Most of society today values gold in nothing more than a materialistic way and views it as simply an attractive yellow metal that is worth a significant of money. If one does some research into its unique properties they realize that gold may be one of the most important elements in the universe, as it will always remain eternal. Gold is the only material that allows a frequency to pass through without being disrupted. It also has incredible heat reflective properties and never corrodes. We use gold in virtually all of our electronics such as computers and cell phones. Travel in space itself may not be possible without the aid of gold. Society is just discovering the true potential of what gold can do. It may even extend life and repair a planet's atmosphere. As strange as that sounds, it shows why a civilization would be interested in going to great lengths to acquire it.

Planet Earth contains the large volumes of gold in our solar system, with the highest concentrations being found around South Africa. There have been thousands, if not millions of ancient mining sites discovered there, all showing direct evidence of metal smelting, mining, and habitation, long before our history books are willing to admit. All of this information is carefully kept quiet and suppressed from society. It is no coincidence that archaeologists have discovered some of our earliest human ancestors out of South Africa. It may be a separate cradle of humankind, along with what is now Iraq and Syria. Consider where much of the war and instability has revolved around over the last 20 years. The ancient land of Babylon is still being fought over thousands of years later by the elite echelons of society who wish to control the past.

There was an important need to acquire large amounts of gold out of the Earth by digging deep shafts underground in what was known as the Abzu. After thousands of years of labor, the exhausted Igigi miners working for the Anunnaki revolted and demanded relief. The Anunnaki head scientist on Earth known as Enki lobbied the council to use the primitive hominid beings they had found while surveying, known as Denisovan or Neanderthals. The Anunnaki desperately needed to find another source of labor to satisfy the grueling work in the Abzu to acquire gold for their dwindling atmosphere. After extensive moral thought, it was decided to use the native hominid species as primitive workers in the mines and increase their intelligence. Through their vast understanding of DNA manipulation, the Anunnaki decided to alter the genome of the native pre-hominid species already present on the planet with their own DNA to create modern day Homo sapiens. After much trial and error, an adequate version was created that fit the needs of the work.

During the creation of our species, disagreements arose between the powerful two brothers known as Enki, (Poseidon) and Enlil, (Zeus) over the allowance of free will and intelligence within Homo sapiens. Enki and Enlil were the bloodline sons of Anu, which combines to form the name Anunnaki. These brothers were given ownership and responsibility over planet Earth and deemed themselves gods of everything beneath them. Enki was highly skilled in genetics and with the help of his sister Ninhursag (Isis), created modern day Homo sapiens and allowed the ability for free will within them. We should always remember that there are two sides to every story and must move past simple linear thinking to explain everything.

The original purpose behind the creation of Homo sapiens, through the eyes of Enlil, was to become a simple slave race with only enough intelligence to comprehend basic orders. Even the idea of giving humans more intelligence through splicing their own DNA greatly angered Enlil and he fiercely opposed it. Unbeknownst to Enlil, his half-brother Enki ended up designing a model of Homo sapien that was far too intelligent and could rival even their greatness as a species. Enki felt great responsibility and compassion for his creation and endowed Homo sapiens with an advanced brain and higher consciousness like that of their own. This new model proved very troublesome during work in the mines because of its high intellect and constant disobedience. When Enlil found out that Enki had given humanity the gifts of their intelligence and right to free will through consciousness expansion he was furious and promised to enslave humanity forever and never allow them to know the Truth of who they are.

When Enlil was chosen to be the ruler of Earth, instead of his half-brother Enki, a promise that had been made for the ultimate slavery of humanity was orchestrated and carried out. The famous Garden of Eden story speaks to these decisions made for humanity through Adam and Eve and the metaphorical use of a serpent and god figure. The decision given to Adam and Eve from the serpent, about whether or not they should eat from the tree of knowledge of good and evil, led to their banning from the garden known as Eden, which is located in Iraq where the Tigris and Euphrates Rivers meet. The clever trick used by organized religion is to make society believe that the serpent is evil and that the god figure is divine and assisting humanity. This crucial teaching describing the enslavement of humanity is written around the two brothers of Enlil and Enki, represented here as God and the serpent.

In the story of Adam and Eve, God, or Enlil, doesn't want humanity to know of good or evil, but to instead live in complete ignorance and darkness of the Truth. Adam and Eve ultimately decided they want free will, thanks to the sacrifices made from Enki, known as the serpent. Enlil banishes Homo sapiens to a life of bondage and slavery and through the creation of warfare and money, tricked humanity into an eternal slumber. The overall scope of control and suppression to society all stems back from the original anger felt by Enki's gifts for free will within humanity.

To avoid uprisings and understanding their true history, humans were kept in a state of total amnesia from the past. The human genome was altered so that it would function in a much slower frequency, blocking off our consciousness expansion. The double helix of the human DNA and chakra system was split apart and unplugged to prevent our awareness. This alteration of human genes caused our true potential and most of our divine gifts to be kept secret from our perception. Human beings were the perfect control species since we desperately feared our own mortality. That fear is the primary means for our continued domination and brutally violent past.

Human beings are now beginning to wake up and learn the Truth of this identity which was stolen from us through thousands of years of slavery. Such a notion may be uncomfortable for some to consider, but like all great stories, ours is merely just beginning. The keys to understanding who humans beings really are lies within the knowledge passed down by the great designers of our species. Evidence for this design can be found throughout the pyramids of Egypt and in nearly every significant past culture before us. Detailed artwork depicted into stone, tells the story of where the creators of humanity came from. This same story is echoed all throughout ancient cultures across the planet that were separated by enormous distances and completely cut off from one another.

The most overwhelming evidence that proves the existence of ancient teachers to early mankind can be seen very clearly when further inspecting the great pyramids of Giza. From the point of an objective observer looking at these pyramids from above, they will immediately notice that the geometric alignments follows a strict pattern, found similarly with other pyramids all over the world. Since modern history tries to convince us that the great pyramids of Giza were made by a relatively primitive society, the calculations and precise planning needed for these alignments would have been completely impossible.

The orientation of these great pyramids on Earth exactly mirrors the placement of the stars in Orion's Belt. This similar theme can be found with ancient pyramid structures all over the planet. This integral design utilizes the Earth's natural energy centers to create a healing and knowledge center. By uniquely designing the pyramids to mimic the harmonic frequency of human beings, we can now begin to understand why the largest structures on Earth were created. These enormous healing centers were used by the ancient blood line pharaohs of Egypt to extend their life as long as possible and rule the people who worshiped them. This ancient bloodline is the key to the true identity of who these pharaohs of Egypt really were. By breeding with humans, the pharaohs of Egypt were the direct decedents of the Anunnaki. Thousands of years later, this practice of inbreeding and the obsession over bloodlines shows the intrinsic need of these ancient visitors to preserve their DNA.

Further evidence for these visitors can be clearly seen in the largest of these pyramids known as Khufu, where there are two important rooms which were built called the King and Queen's Chambers. These large chambers represent the embodiment of Osiris and Isis on Earth and their worship from the human race. They provide detailed star maps showing the precise locations behind the ancient lineage of the past. The King's chamber contains two long vertical shafts, which align exactly with the constellations of Orion and Alpha Draconis during the winter solstice of that time period. Alpha Draconis is revered as the original North Star before Polaris replaced it in modern times. Beside the Kings Chamber lies the Queens Chamber, which also contains two long vertical shafts which point directly to the stars of Sirius and Ursa Minor. These ancient star alignments honor the many realms of the 'gods' who came from beyond Earth and the unique symbolism found within each chamber speaks volumes to our forgotten history.

The underlying Truth hidden beneath this knowledge is that the Anunnaki are the direct descendants and incarnations of the legendary king and queen of ancient Egyptian culture known as Osiris and Isis (Enki and Ninhursag). It's clear to me that because the Anunnaki and many other past cultures worshipped the locations of Sirius and Orion in pyramids and megalithic structures all across the planet, it's therefore likely that these beings are simply part of a greater Orion and Sirian Empire. This grand hierarchy system of vastly advanced civilizations controlling those below them and an intergalactic reality hidden all around us is beyond humbling to become aware of and realize you are part of.

The ancient Egyptians worshiped the Anunnaki because of the deep Truth for what their species had contributed long ago to the

DNA of the human race. Developing humans were given great amounts of information from the various 'gods' that were visiting and residing here. This crossing of human and Anunnaki DNA led to what we know of as the great kings and pharaohs of much of the ancient world. In Egypt, there is overwhelming evidence showing this forgotten influence, with drawings and depictions of tall enlarged craniums, and animal-like symbolic appearances. So much of this information has been used in metaphors in various religious texts and stories echoed throughout our history. All of these depictions were simply showing the bloodline kings and queens who ruled over human society. The Sumerian King's List verifies the Truth behind this model of society when it says, "When kingship was lowered from heaven", giving proof to its origins and the extended reins of its rulers.

The largest structures ever built on Earth give us compelling evidence for this worship of the creators of mankind. With the flimsy reasoning given to us for the purpose of the construction of these great pyramids, supposedly as the burial chambers for the Pharaohs, it should be clearly noted that not one pharaoh has **ever** been found in a large pyramid. The nearby Valley of the King's was their burial site. This trick is a very clever way to lead the public away from the true purpose of these incredible structures and how they were built.

The great pyramids of Giza are found in very precise locations across the planet and utilize the Earth's natural energy centers which we are just now beginning to understand. Think of the medical and healing marvels that await humanity in the future if we decide to move forward as a species. Instead of always looking towards the future to learn, we should instead look back at what the ancients were trying to show us all along. Everything we need to know about ourselves can be found in the lost echoes of the past.

To fully understand the entire story of us, we must now move the narrative back to around 20,000 years ago. We observe that tremendous change has occurred within human society in a very short time. Mankind is able to temporarily thrive in some places with the absence of Enlil's dark hand of control on the planet. A complete forgotten chapter of human time occurred, wiped from our memories like amnesia. Advanced cultures like the Atlanteans and Lemurians became pinnacles of what we think of as a utopian society. Yet these advanced human cultures existed far before modern archaeology gives credit for. The timeline current history feeds to us presents a slowly developing human species still using only primitive tools and discovering fire. This grossly misinterpreted timeline is used to cover up our true history and the extensive extraterrestrial influences from the past. Whether you like the idea of not, we are certainly not alone in the universe.

During this lost time period existed the ancient Atlanteans and Lemurian people, who constructed enormous monolithic structures, towering over thriving cities, built along some the warmer regions of the planet. All of this advancement and scientific understanding was only possible from the influences of the Anunnaki and others who have traveled here. This period of the human timeline was greatly accelerated far beyond the normal evolutionary means. We know of this information from the ancient Egyptians and the destroyed library of Alexandria. The idea that advanced civilizations thrived this far back is laughable to most archaeologist and mainstream scientists. That fate of linearity is due to a complete lack of understanding our connections and influences all along, by those who came from the stars.

This time period on Earth was known as the Pleistocene Epoch when the last great ice age covered the planet. The North American and Eurasian Continent were covered in up to two miles of ice. Enormous animals like wooly mammoths and saber-toothed tigers roamed the northern regions, while most of the human civilizations lived in the warmer coastal areas. The water that is present on Earth now is nearly the same amount that has been here for millions of years. During the last ice age, vast amounts of water were locked up in the ice and this caused sea levels all over the Earth to be 400 feet lower than they are today. Many advanced civilizations developed along the coasts, much like our current model is today with large cities. The human species had made tremendous leaps to where some technologies and understanding were far advanced of where even we are today. These technologies were derived by using frequency, vibration and an extensive knowledge of the cosmos. Ancient remnants of these cities can be seen all over the Earth, submerged and forgotten under hundreds of feet of seawater. These lost cities that are just being discovered are completely re-writing our history. Today, even with all of the modern technology we have available to us, humans have only mapped and explored about 10% of the ocean bottom. Imagine all of the other incredible lost pinnacles of civilization which still remain hidden beneath the forbidden depths of the ocean.

It can be easy to simply pretend that all of this is just science fiction and an elaborate story in order to avoid the difficulties that come along with this narrative, but we cannot look away any longer. The Truth is we don't have any more time to continue pretending. Our very future depends on expanding our awareness before we too disappear like so many cultures before us. Knowledge is truly power and is the fuel for all conscious expansion. We have a fundamental right as a free populace to not allow the hijacking of our history any longer. I intend to rectify that blunder and provide only Truth.

One of the smoking guns of modern Truth can be found once again when looking at the existing monolithic structures present in Egypt. Humanity, with all of its seemingly advanced technology, has been given the illusion of its greatness through accumulated ego. This illusion has blinded us from seeing what is right in front of our eyes all along. When we look at the largest created structures on Earth, like the great pyramids of Giza, we simply assume that we could also create them as well. Even today, with all of the high-tech, modern machinery available to us, humans still could **not** build the pyramids of Egypt. Yet, this concept is barely considered, or even discussed openly. If the Truth behind these incredibly detailed designs came out, it would change the way we view history forever.

The advanced precision used to build the great pyramid of Khufu incorporates detailed measurements from which the Earth's size and shape can be perfectly calculated. What that means is that builders of this great pyramid knew the specific dimensions for planet Earth. The pyramid of Khufu is a literal representation of the Earth itself, lining up to specific compass points like an enormous sundial. The precise ratios represented by the construction of the pyramid of Khufu, show a far advanced knowledge that could only have come from an intelligent, extraterrestrial species. Yet, even in all of its grandeur, humanity is still far more willing to accept that the great accomplishments of the distant past were done by a nomadic tribe of humans, utilizing nothing more than primitive tools. The largest structures ever made on Earth are sitting right in plain sight and yet most of society ignores the importance of them completely.

So much of human history and what was lost from it has been shrouded in mystery for hundreds of years. Entire advanced cultures seemed to disappear overnight, which left much of the clues to their origins lost to history forever. Archaeologist are now finding significant evidence that is showing that the Earth suffered a series of devastating space impacts and even a pole shift that nearly wiped out the entire human species. This evidence can be seen widely distributed in soil layers all over the world and referenced in many religious texts. The soil layers describe to us a series of large cosmic strikes that slammed into the northern hemisphere ice caps and land masses in the late Pleistocene era, roughly 12,800 years ago. The evidence for the magnitude of these extinction level events can be seen clearly from within the impacted soil layers, which have shown high levels of nuclear glass, nanodiamonds, and thick ash in their deposits. So what could have caused these disasters?

This important new evidence shows a direct correlation back to the findings of Robert Harrington and Thomas Van Flandern around the influences that Planet X may have had on the Kuiper Belt long ago. According to their research, a new planet in our outer solar system called Planet X may periodically disrupt asteroids and comets in the Kuiper Belt, sending them hurling towards Earth. This connection back to our hidden history is shedding much light for helping to piece together a plausible timeline that describes a mass extinction of "biblical" proportions. These new facts finally fit together to explain why so many advanced cultures from all over the world simply vanished. During this time period, the Earth was much colder and ice caps across our northern land masses were up to two miles deep. It's hard to try and even wrap our heads around that staggering figure. The famous Empire State Building in New York City only measures about 1,200 feet tall. Try and imagine these enormous ice caps being 5 to 10 times that tall and covering almost entire continents.

Ice core samples from Greenland show startling evidence that around 12,800 years ago an asteroid or comet may have greatly impacted the planet. Debris from this comet or asteroid slammed into the Earth's icecaps and northern landmasses, resulting in trillions of gallons of water being released in a very short time. Envision a wave of water and ice sweeping across much of the northern hemisphere devastating the human civilizations and mega-fauna living there. These cosmic impacts on the Earth spread a plume of ash and dust that led to a plunge in global temperatures. With this disastrous flood went much of our knowledge and understanding of this time period which was simply washed away in a torrent of boulders and meltwater. Dramatic scarring can still be seen all across the northern hemisphere, especially in locations such as Washington or Idaho in the United States, where mountainsides display the impressive ripple effects left behind from this turbulent river of ice and water.

Across nearly every major culture on planet we see overwhelming evidence describing a massive flood that occurred throughout human history, including this powerful quote from Genesis 7:19-20, "And the waters prevailed exceedingly upon the Earth; and all of the high hills, that were under the whole heaven, were covered". The most famous depiction of this great flood can be seen in the biblical story of Noah, whose name in the Sumerian King List was Ubara-Tutu. Instead of heavy rain, it was a wall of water from a sudden pole shift that caused a devastating extinction of mammals and human populations across the Earth. Noah, who was also known as Atrahasis, was saved to protect the important Rh- DNA within him and his family and was guided secretly by his father Enki.

Instead of sending us back into an ice age, Earth experienced a run-away warming effect with lasted for thousands of years. This stunning and dramatic change to the climate was brought on by disastrous volcanic eruptions, earthquakes, and entire land masses submerging beneath turbulent oceans. The combination of these two events would forever change the climate and species on the planet. What was a much colder place to survive in previously would lead to the warmer Holocene and a new chapter in mankind's history.

Ice core samples from Greenland have given us a picture that leaves most climatologists scratching their heads in confusion without connecting this information with the ancient past. The extreme warming that occurred on Earth, coupled with soil layers showing thick volcanic ash laid down during the same time period speaks volumes to these cosmic cataclysms and gravity disruptions of the planet. This new window into our past is only made possible by the brave researchers like Graham Hancock and Zecharia Sitchin, willing to find this evidence and challenge the entire narrative. The fact that our true history and unlocking the secrets of who we are is being found and told by only a handful of researchers and archaeologists, shows you how controlled the view of history really is. If not for these brave minds where would we end up?

In the years leading up to the end of the Younger Dryas period, the Earth was warming at a rapid rate. Severe climate change triggered enormous wildfires that blotted out the sun and led to extensive droughts creating hostile desert environments, wiping out the forests that previously existed there. The Earth's climate was transformed into a much warmer planet after these events. The few places that were spared of this cataclysm, including much of Africa, is the main reason why so many large animals still exist there today. These mega-fauna all over the northern hemisphere were wiped out, leaving only the smaller mammals who were able to seek shelter underground. Vast caverns of bones have been found all over the northern regions, showing the quickly shifting climate conditions that led to these mass extinctions of mammals.

It was during this violent period coming out of the Younger Dryas, that the philosopher Plato gives the same date for the famous, lost city of Atlantis being destroyed by earthquakes and volcano eruptions, leading to the entire landmass submerging into rising oceans. This incredibly advanced culture, with everything they achieved, was lost into the sea and made into a fairy tale in modern times. Much of what we consider just silly stories may actually be recorded accounts by those trying to explain this tragedy and violent history preceding us.

The Anunnaki who remained on the Earth survived the space cataclysms by taking shelter in enormous excavated cave networks or leaving the planet's orbit. In fact, regardless of the temperature profile found on the surface, it seems very evident that many of these Anunnaki prefer living underground. This continuously repetitive theme has come up over and over while researching and has strongly pointed to a clear indication for the presence of vast hidden cave networks all over the planet. As preposterous as this may sound, countless abandoned and underground complexes have already been found whose number is increasing with every new discovery made.

The most famous of these discoveries occurred in Turkey in 1963, when a secret door in a wall revealed itself to be Derinkuyu, a colossal underground city that was estimated to have a capacity of more than 20,000 people. Further exploration of the site revealed a vast network of tunnels which all interconnected to a lost underground world. Why would so much work have been done to live underground and how would they have known what was coming from space? The answer to those questions points to the overwhelming evidence that those who dwelled within these caves simply was not human. The sheer scope of work involved in these elaborate projects would have been a monumental effort without some dire need for their construction. This important clue, connecting with the new evidence showing the devastating space impacts on the Earth at the time, begins to formulate a narrative for these forgotten visitors.

The cave networks we have discovered today have been long abandoned and seem to have been only used to survive the extinction events of the past. With the technology to create these elaborate but temporary living quarters, it must be recognized that far more advanced cave networks were created as permanent dwellings for those who remained behind. The fate of humanity was left to a small and dwindled number of individuals, scattered across the warmer parts of our planet and mostly confined to Africa and parts of the Middle East. The entire human species nearly went extinct in the blink of an eye. With all of the past technology and knowledge totally lost to us it truly was a reset button in our timeline. Mankind was back to being hunters and gatherers as we slowly worked our way up the evolutionary chain, completely unaware of anything preceding us.

Taking advantage of this unique opportunity in our timeline, it was decided by some of the Anunnaki who were left to govern this planet that they would physiologically enslave humanity by creating an enormous system of control to keep the population suppressed and distracted from the Truth. We are that consciously developing human species waking up at this moment to shockingly discover that we have been living in a matrix of slavery for thousands of years. This new found level of awareness can be overwhelming and extremely shocking to realize. So many unknown questions remain still regarding this time period and fully understanding those who traveled here. What we do know is found scattered in ancient text and dusty scrolls, describing an advanced group of beings known as the Anunnaki who rule over Earth.

Through a dark collaboration with other beings, the Enlil branch of the Anunnaki lords in charge of Earth secretly formed what would later become known as the 13 families of the Illuminati, or Cabal, thousands of years later. They allowed the implementation of a detailed system of conscious slavery that still firmly holds humanity in an illusion of reality. This complex system of suppressing consciousness is completely dependent on Truth remaining hidden from our awareness. The direct influences from these visitors tampering in our history, by the utilization of advanced manipulation techniques for the control of perceived reality, is what has shaped our society to what it is today. Our timeline represents a coerced future that has been designed for us to live in.

Evidence for their influence and purpose can be seen infused in the countless monolithic structures scattered throughout the ancient world from Central America, to the South Pacific. These ancient human cultures worshiped the Anunnaki, known to them as "gods," for the important gifts they provided them which propelled their developing society. From the incredible mathematic precision behind the design of the pyramids to the crumbling ruins of ancient cities, these intrinsically important achievements from ancient cultures provide all the answers to the Truth behind these visitors. The legacy they left behind has been passed down for centuries by native peoples through the use of storytelling and elaborate artwork describing those who came from the stars long ago.

Factions from within each controlling group of the 13 bloodline families created a complex system to infiltrate all forms of finance, energy, and politics in society. Control of these vital areas was important for maintaining social stability and order within the human farm. This agenda was coordinated and carried out by a small loyal group of powerful family bloodline members, living in ultimate secrecy alongside developing humans. Working up through the ranks of influencing and controlling powerful military societies like the Romans, they carried the symbol of Christianity, represented by the mighty Red Cross. A loyal group of the bloodline families, backed by the authoritarian empire of the Christian church, would establish what would later become known as the Knights Templar, whose legacy would be written about for ages. This unstoppable elite group of knights, claiming to be sent by "God," devastated and murdered thousands in their obsession to reclaim the Holy land. This ancient alliance and promise can still be seen today with the overwhelming military support given to the government of Israel.

The 13 bloodline families of the Illuminati order carried out a complex agenda that is finally nearing its conclusion. It can be clearly seen on the back of an American dollar bill with the unfinished pyramid and the all-seeing eye. The important use of the number 13 can be seen cleverly hidden within symbols all across governments and found throughout printed currency. This reoccurring number represents the 13 families of the Illuminati who maintain and run every part of society. Some of this material can be hard to absorb or even to believe, but in many examples like this, the symbols are right out in the open, hiding in plain sight. These ancient symbols speak directly to the sinister agenda which has been planned for all along with a One World Government. This Orwellian agenda has been attempted over and over in our society and has been rejected when the population eventually discovers the Truth in its control. Each time this attempt is made, the formula is modified in order to find a balance between perceived freedoms and those which are removed.

The Illuminati are a network of 13 immensely wealthy family members who control virtually everything on the Earth. This is represented clearly when looking at the one dollar bill in the United States. As a reoccurring theme, each group of symbols on the one dollar bill add up to precisely 13. From the number of stairs leading up the all-seeing pyramid to the number of stars represented above the eagle, the symbolism present on the one dollar bill is overwhelming when one has their eyes open. Beyond just money, these secret symbols hiding in plain site can be found all over the world. People stroll by the Vatican of Rome or

Washington Monument in D.C., casually taking pictures and are completely unaware of the elaborate framework of complex architecture that surrounds them. When these city designs are viewed from above, they reveal precisely created pentagrams and unique symbology, which often represents specific star constellations. The archaic worship of these long forgotten owners of Earth is still occurring to this day. The majority of the public is simply too naive to realize and connect these Truths because of our inability to see outside the box. The easiest way to hide a secret is to put it right out in the open and make it a joke.

The head of the Illuminati ruling families can be commonly identified throughout the ages and traced back by following their ancient family crest with the double-headed eagle. Whatever civilization bore the mighty eagle as its crest went on to become a warring super power. The ancient battle between the eagle and serpent has raged for thousands of years as the gods of Zeus and Poseidon fight over mankind's civilizations. The Rothschild crest is always dominated by the color red, with a secondary color of blue. In German, "red shield" directly means "Rotschild," which became later known as the Rothschild family dynasty. This ancient family has been inbreeding and only marrying within the family for thousands of years to protect the purity of the bloodline. Think back all throughout human history, to nearly every successful military conquering society of the world, from the Romans to the Egyptians, and see the constant theme showing inbreeding as a means of securing important DNA traits. This inbreeding and the deep secrecy within these families simply cannot be ignored any longer and shows the important connections back to their ancient roots, now thought of as just a myth by society.

With such expansive knowledge over the relatively simple minded population of humans, it was no challenge working up to the highest influences of power through the lust of money. Human beings were far too busy surviving and raising families and processed almost no access to higher learning. Knowledge and information simply wasn't readily available and those who came of it were simply murdered or threatened when they became a problem. By infiltrating religion, government and all forms of power, these secret families worked their way up throughout history to eventually control the entire planet and every human living on it. This information is almost impossible to comprehend unless you understand the entire story and how everything fits together.

The Rothschild family dynasty was able to achieve global domination by their direct funding and monetary support for each side of a war. There was far more money to make in war then there was in peace, especially if you can create and fund the conflicts. The family's unimaginable wealth, in excess of hundreds of trillions of dollars, is almost unmeasurable to most minds. Much of the Truths for how sinister this family really was may never be fully known to us, as very little has been allowed to be released containing their full biography. Described as extremely experienced bankers, their unusually extensive knowledge into money made them very successful in the collaboration and combining of all major world banks.

The ancient purpose for this family can still be seen in the ownership of billions of dollars in gold bullion, stored in secure banking states like those of Switzerland. This neutrally created state is entirely owned by the banking center of the family. During planning, a country was needed which could be considered neutral from war and not be at risk of losing the vast amounts of wealth stored in its banking system. Since the value of money is largely irrelevant, the true definition of wealth was in the value of gold. For hundreds of years, the price of gold on Earth has been determined by the Rothschild family. Owning enormous mines all over the world, this quench for gold stems from the very reason they were here in the first place. Even today, the Rothschild family still determines the daily price of gold. This evidence shows a direct link for how this family has been able to control and manipulate currency and prices for centuries. In understanding the reasons for these actions and their obsession with gold, it can be traced back to the original purpose of those who traveled here thousands of years ago.

The Rothschild dynasty represents the direct link between the Anunnaki who came here and the important bloodline crosses between human beings, which has occurred since before the time of the Egyptians. This overwhelmingly common theme gives direct evidence for why the bloodline obsession is so intrinsically important to these families. Many of our political leaders and rulers can all be directly traced back to this royal bloodline connection. This preservation of unique DNA traits within a human being is critical for their ability to act out such cruel and inhumane practices. When we look back at the sheer brutality of some of these leaders, it begins to become more clear as to the reasons behind their madness. Considered "royal" blood, these kings and queens still sit on the throne in modern day countries like England and Saudi Arabia.

The head of the Rothschild family in Europe was Mayer Amschel Rothschild, who was then proceeded by his five sons. Mayer Amschel was an expert in banking practices and learned these valuable skills from Jacob Wolf Oppenheimer. Remember the name Jacob Wolf Oppenheimer, for it will come up generations later in the United States. Mayer Amschel Rothschild passed on this knowledge of banking and finances to his five sons, who were each sent to important cities in England, Italy, Germany, France, and Austria in order to establish independent branches representing the family. Each of these important European countries was chosen based on their influences over the region and the world. The Rothschild's knew that the key to controlling a countries affairs is directly through the ownership of its banking sector.

In the United States, this bloodline branch of the family is famously known as the Rockefellers, who own and control large amounts of money and land. In order to secure monetary control and power, the Rockefeller family, under the close eye of the Rothschild's, created a privately owned banking subsidiary called the Federal Reserve, with the help of President William Howard Taft and Woodrow Wilson. Instead of having a government run operation, the use of this privately owned central bank could determine all finances and monetary control over every faction of our society. The fact that the supposedly sovereign United States is run by a privately owned bank by the Rothschild's, gives strong evidence for individual governing bodies being nothing more than an empty shell for this control. Those who control the money of the planet completely dictate the actions of every individual underneath them.

The most notable secret society which emerged out of the ancient Illuminati families was the Freemasons. This fraternal branch of the ancient bloodlines included notable members such as presidents George Washington, Harry Truman and William Howard Taft. You will begin to see that all of this is connected and part of the agenda of the Illuminati. In all, 14 United States presidents have been confirmed as being Freemasons. One of the most important aspects to understand for what defines membership in the Freemasonry is the notion of being an illuminated mind. That means that upon acceptance into this secret society, you will be given advanced knowledge and Truth which has been kept from the general population. To become illuminated simply means to be enlightened with information. That stark reality gives further evidence to show the massive suppression of information used to control humanity.

Along with the powerful Freemasons, another far more secretive society has quietly been worshiped by powerful leaders for generations, called the Skull and Bones Society. The very notion that many of our political leaders and those in places of power are attending a worship of the dark occult is extremely unsettling and unbelievable to most. I can assure you, this information is very real and as disturbing as it may be, gives clarity to much of the Truth that has gone on right under our noses. In this grand technological age, all one has to do is search for Bohemian Grove and do a little research to verify and see for yourself this information.

Many of our well known United States presidents and countless other world leaders have come to this secret retreat to pledge their loyalty towards these ruling elite families of the Illuminati. Located in the redwood forests of California, this elite clubs entrance is adorned by a large gate emblazoned with a skull and bones in the center. These markings give further evidence for the credibility of these secret organizations. Bohemian Grove is a private, invitation-only gathering place, featuring extensive seating around a large bonfire, with flames that light up an enormous satanic owl looming behind it. No cameras or recording devices are ever allowed in and security around the area is heavily guarded. The only pictures and information we have to justify these claims can be found from those who managed to smuggle out photographs obtained from membership pamphlets.

The essential goal of this secret organization is a mock sacrifice and indoctrination into this satanic society. If you look back all through history, sacrifice has been a regular theme in so many of the more sinister cultures predating us. This obsession with blood sacrifice is the overlying theme which seems to rule these secret societies under the Illuminati. I only wish to inform you of the Truth and ask that you see how real all of this is for yourself.

Some of the most famous and influential members of the Skull and Bones society included well-known names like Bush, Ford, and even Oppenheimer. The full list is long and we may never know how far back this secret cult society has actually gone. I find it incredibly fascinating and somewhat alarming, that so many of our political leaders and even the designers of weapons of mass destruction, were all members of the Skull and Bones society. The famous Julius Robert Oppenheimer, a direct bloodline descendant from Jacob Wolf Oppenheimer, was a prominent member of this secret society. Furthermore, the infamous Manhattan Project planning was held at Bohemian Grove in 1942, in which Julius Robert Oppenheimer was integral in the development of the atomic bomb. Think of the vast consequences perpetrated on humanity because of this secret meeting. None of this is a coincidence and shows the finite connections found between these ancient bloodline members all along. Whatever your predetermined conclusions for this information are, these connections simply cannot be ignored any longer and provide windows to the Truth.

When trying to understand the purpose of these secret organizations under the Illuminati, we must first consider why these particular men were chosen in the first place and what each one represented on a global scale. If we look at the three names mentioned above for Bush, Ford, and Oppenheimer, a clear picture begins to emerge which shows the domination over world politics, energy, and war. Remember, there are no such things as coincidences, only the illusion of them. You begin to realize that nearly every aspect of our timeline has been shaped by their collaboration for control. Our planet, our home, has been devastated by these monsters, who have stripped much of its natural resources and heavily polluted the minds of the people. Blocked at every turn in history, the Truth is that our society would be completely running on clean and sustainable energy already if not for this alternate future that has been forced to occur. Instead of looking at the past world events as random, we must see them for what they really are, a designed future for us following an agenda.

Indoctrination in this society within the Illuminati gives fame and wealth but with a steep price. It is the same thing that has been happening for thousands of years with bribing and allowing power in exchange for freedom. This may sound like an elaborate movie plot but I assure you this is very real, and direct evidence can be clearly seen for who attends these Bohemian Grove events and who then succeeds and finds wealth and fame. It has become a joke in our culture, as have many of the Truths seemingly right out in the open.

The Illuminati, comprising the major ruling elite families, became the controllers of all finances, war, and major activities across the Earth. World politics, completely infiltrated and bought, used propaganda to spread fear and instability across the planet, keeping humans in a constant, stagnant state. These politicians and leaders are normally nothing more than an empty shell, willing to do just enough to not have mass unrest. We receive just enough "freedom" to have the illusion that we are free.

In the last speech that the great John F. Kennedy gave before he was silenced, he spoke extensively about these secret societies and those who control all world affairs. He wished to rid the planet of this cancer which has spread to every corner of humanity and finally bring freedom to the people. In his last statement he said, "Man will be what he was born to be: free and independent". That sentence speaks volumes for what the Illusion of Us really represents at its core. The underlying Truth in all of this is that by becoming fully aware you also become free as well. Freedom does not simply end at physical chains but on every facet of what makes us human. Not even presidents are out of the reach for these secret societies, which all make up the Illuminati.

A critical component when understanding the relationship between governments and the secret societies that ultimately control them is through the selective basis for which information is provided to the individual, which is determined by their level of clearance to it. What that means is that even high ranking members of government, including most presidents, do not have access to some of the most classified levels of this privileged information. In most cases these high-ranking military generals are not even aware that they are merely pawns beneath a secret Shadow

Government which maintains the agenda of the Illuminati.

The Shadow Government, which functions under the veil of ultimate secrecy, operates large, underground secure facilities, where they utilize and work with advanced technology. Through a secret agreement signed between the US government and the Anunnaki in 1954, an exchange of advanced technology was given to them under strict stipulations. This disastrous decision led to the complete hijacking of democracy in the United States and much of the world. It was the final nail in the coffin for our free planet. This treaty led to the complete takeover of health, education, and politics in society. Many of the suppressions of our consciousness that have slowed our expansion can be derived from this decision.

Most of what we consider to be brilliant inventions that propel society forward are nothing more than the outdated technology that is allowed to the public. Many brilliant inventors, like Nikola Tesla, have seen their work completely destroyed, or in some cases, the individual is even murdered in order to silence them. Since new technology has the ability to rapidly transform our awareness, it had to be controlled and maintained. Trillions of dollars were funneled into these underground facilities, through the monopolized banking networks of the Rothschild family dynasty. By seizing control of all monetary systems across nearly every major country of the world, these secret societies have been able to dictate almost every single social and political decision that has been made.

The ultimate goal of the Shadow Government is to maintain and continue the agenda of the ancient bloodlines of the Illuminati, who seek to finally establish a New World Order. The unfinished pyramid and the all-seeing eye on the one dollar bill, directly give evidence for this secret agenda for humanity. That is how so many political leaders and high-ranking military personnel are still nothing more than puppets being dangled from a string of their own awareness. We are bound by only what we understand and everything outside of that perception is considered not real to us. Humanity must wake up to who the real owners of our supposed democracy really are.

A special task group was created within the government whose purpose was to directly work with the elite families and those who they report to. This unique committee still meets today and is called the Bilderberg Group. The Bilderberg Group, which even includes the president of the United States and most of the powerful leaders in the world, meet every year to discuss how to control and maintain the release of information to the public. These secret society meetings are held out in the open with false titles hiding their true purpose. The easiest way to keep a secret is to put it out in the open as a joke so that it will be immediately discredited.

The scope and magnitude of this immense design for controlling resources and human beings is the key to understanding the matrix of our conscious control. There is an old saying that says "follow the money," and it couldn't be more Truthful here. Following this dirty money trail allows us to glimpse the dark underbelly to reality, where elite trillionaires directly fund each side of brutal conflicts in order to maintain instability and profit gain. By financially supporting each side of a war, the Rothschild family dynasty is able to ensure the success of human depopulation, control of consciousness through fear and tremendous monetary gains. On her deathbed, Amschel Mayer Rothschild's wife nonchalantly stated. "If my sons did not want wars, there would be none". This powerful statement not only exposes the Truth behind the financial influences on events but on the systematic eradication of hundreds of millions of human beings throughout history.

To gain valuable perspective on our current situation we must recognize the insurmountable loss of human life that has been engineered on us through created genocide. Feel for a moment the tragic sadness from more than a billion screams becoming silenced in only a few thousand years. These parasites of humanity have profited from our deaths for far too long and left in their wake despair so deep it has ruined entire generations of people. Humanity was driven to this madness through confusion and anger, derived from the worship of hijacked religions for control. It became enough to kill a man in the name of the so-called "god" who they represented. This tragic ideology and our lust for wealth has led to more murder and genocide than any other means in human history.

A staggering 60 million people were killed in World War II alone, which was allowed to rampage across nearly the entire planet. This horrifying extermination of humanity was done for means of depopulation, eradication of the Jewish people, and the agenda for how the world was to be broken up and governed. Considered to be nothing more than a simple chess match to the elites by utilizing humanity's leftover barbarism, the ruling Illuminati families sent millions to be slaughtered for nothing more than entertainment, money and total control through fear. One should think for a moment what the Earth would be like if the Nazis had been victorious in their multiple attempts at global domination. The future would have been a terrifying draconian society, with all freedoms stripped away from even the meager few we are given now. Human beings have commonly been viewed by the elite bloodline families as nothing more than troublesome, unevolved mammals, who are residing on their planet.

The collection of bloodline families makes up what we know of as the Illuminati and maintains total order across all of society. The advanced visitors know that through extended periods of peace, great expansion can be sought by humanity. They know that the only way to maintain total control of the population is through the creation of terror and fear. If the population begins to reject war then false flag attacks are created to fill the void. False flag attacks are an artificially planned attack which intends to give the perception that our patriotic freedoms are in jeopardy.

The built up effect of this designed anger, frustration and hate, almost snowballed into the total destruction of humanity from nuclear weapons. We may never know how close we really came to that nightmare scenario. Coming out of the brief aftermath of the last world war, society was immediately thrown into the grips of fear once again from the Cold War and the increasing threats from a nuclear holocaust. The idea of allowing peace for humanity is simply not an option for those who control society and refuse to give up the rights to this planet. Years and years of seemingly being on the edge of nuclear annihilation has created such hatred and fear across the planet that we almost countdown the remaining time left for our own mutual destruction. We have been at war so long that we don't even know what true peace means any longer. That is the fundamental reason for why war is so heavily funded and alternative energy and education are just on the backburner for the illusion of democracy and freedom here. There is little interest in humanity reaching a peaceful or informed state by many of those still in control.

There continues to be an ongoing attempt at the very top of the pyramid by the controlling families and powerful politicians to continue the agenda for a military society and New World Order. This can be clearly seen from the viewpoint of the Republican Party in the United States and a building up of the military-industrial complex. The core message driven into society is perpetrated through fear and extreme nationalism, neatly wrapped within the illusion of a well-spoken politician. Instead of the context of the message containing substance and new ideas, clever tactics are used to dodge difficult questions, while trying to maintain the image of being a strong leader. This form of deceptive politics has come to define our political processes in the United States. The motivation behind these tactics is to follow the agenda all along and create a military society stripped of individual freedoms. It is no coincidence that this conservative style of politics is represented by the color red as an overwhelming theme.

The overwhelming use of fear and terrorism as a tool, which is constantly coerced into society, is the propaganda needed to continue feeding the enormous military-industrial complex. Without this dark sustenance, there would simply be no means of supporting the hundreds of trillions of dollars needed by the empire of the United States and other military super-powers. One cannot help but draw similar parallels to the downfall of the mighty Roman Empire.

We must ask the hard questions that present themselves to us instead of shying away and continuing to let the status quo dictate our future. We need to expose the sinister purpose for these ancient bloodline family dynasties of interbreeding and secrecy. We must question their obsession with ancient DNA preservation and shed light on the very Truths of ourselves. Why would these families be interested in interbreeding and satanic worship in the 21st century? This almost unimaginable Truth is the real reality hidden around us. As difficult as these concepts are to accept, do not look away from evidence simply because it is hard to consider or stomach. Events we think are wars, terrorist attacks, plagues, and disasters are usually nothing more than spectacles to promote fear and follow a created agenda by the elites. We must not let the dark and depressing means for our control impede our individual path to happiness. We simply accept the past for what it is and move on to changing the future.

The timeline that has occurred for humanity is one that is of sharp contrast to what could have been. Our liberties and freedoms are always being challenged in an ever attempt to finish what was started a long time ago. Politicians have become nothing more than puppet mouthpieces being told what to say based on who directly funds them. The real world that exists behind the curtain of society is made up of nothing more than elite corporate fat cats, owning nearly all of the wealth while the rest of the population simply fights over the scraps. Let all of this information sink in and observe for yourself the Truths in that I speak of. Finding the Truth takes courage while deciding to go back to sleep can seem easy and safe. Remember, ignorance is not bliss it's just lazy. We simply don't have time left to plead ignorance any longer.

This 'Illusion of Us' that has been perpetuated on humanity for thousands of years has caused untold damage to our planet. Most people are unaware of what the byproduct for the 'American dream' has caused us with our unquenchable appetite for empty, material things to fill the void. We must break free of this illusion and finally see the dying world all around us. It is commonly assumed that if extraterrestrial species existed, then the proof would be in their dramatic arrival here and assistance or violence to all of the planet. Seeing our timeline in this very vague way is a symptom of extreme linear thinking. All one has to do is remind themselves of the draconian military society, still gripping onto power over us.

Waking up to the Truth is one of the most difficult things you will ever do in your life. The programming of our reality that has been created to falsely define us is finally beginning to collapse beneath layers of our awakening subconscious. Humanity is beginning to discover that everything in our world we thought was important and defining was simply a clever distraction from the Truth. Trapped in an immense psychopathic lie about everything in our reality, we do the bidding of madness for these rulers unaware of how we are being used. I feel tremendous sadness for the millions who have been killed and sacrificed for nothing more than a game.

What will emerge out of this chaos will be a society hardened by war, deceit and confusion, perpetrated on them for thousands of years. Out of the ashes of the past, we will learn the harsh lessons associated with ignorance and will never again let our freedoms be stolen from all around us. Without these extreme acts of evil and death, we would never fully understand what true peace and love is. The duality of these teachings forms the framework for the ultimate purpose of life in the universe.

Behind this dark shadow that has consumed us there is a beautiful living world which we simply cannot see yet. Human beings are a remarkable species, capable of greatness far beyond the simple narrative we have perceived for ourselves. That hidden potential and the special gifts found deep within our DNA is the reason for all of the turmoil and jealousy on the planet. Simply look at the modern caduceus symbol found in nearly every hospital and medical establishment to see the Truth in what lies ahead for the metamorphosis of our DNA and consciousness. The great secret to our ascension and becoming a being of light lies within achieving the balance within ourselves and expanding our consciousness to understand the intrinsic connections we have with the universe itself. So much of our suppression comes from the mere fear of us waking up to the Truth of everything.

Once the illusion of our current reality breaks and the disclosure of this information finally comes out, it will be like a tidal wave spreading across the planet. Without taking this new information in stages, it will overwhelm even the most gifted minds. Searching within the spiritual self is the key to our own enlightenment and the evolution of humanity. Within the power of the "word," we have the ability to change our own future in the snap of a finger. Freedom only exists from within by those who truly want to seek it. (1, 2, 3, 4, 5, 7, 9, 10, 11, 14, 15)

CHAPTER 3

THE SUPPRESSION OF CONSCIOUSNESS

Let's pretend for a moment you are an extraterrestrial species exploring Earth for the first time. You are able to arrive here because of far advanced technologies and have achieved a balanced and peaceful mindset. You enter our solar system and slowly approach the planet, renowned for its wealth of species and unique ecosystems. As you observe from above, you are appalled by what you see. Much of the planet's forests have been cut down and replaced with sprawling urban centers where air quality can be toxic to breathe at times. Large oil slicks and mountains of garbage conglomerate together in the oceans like artificial islands, creating dead zones where no life can survive. Dirty cities, belching out thick black smoke are crowded with billions of people, all moving like worker drones in nearly uniform apparel. Seeing explosions and gunfire over war- torn areas you quickly reel back in disgust and the first question on your mind is, what happened? The answer to that question can be found here, in understanding how our connection to planet Earth has been completely severed, with our true identity now nothing more than echo lost inside a corrupted, collective mindset.

Before I begin down the story of our suppression, I want to provide a profound quote which perfectly describes the illusion which has enslaved us and blocked off the Truths of our identity. "The ultimate tyranny in a society is not control by martial law, but control by the psychological manipulation of consciousness, through which reality is defined so that those who exist within it, do not even realize they are in prison," -Barbara Marciniak.

The following information on the suppression of humanity and consciousness is not meant to scare you but intended to educate you to the real reality dictating us. Understand that what has been done to our human collective consciousness is a dark story with a very bright ending. The suppression of knowledge and understanding and what it has done to the human species is truly an unsettling concept. Through the control and manipulation of our reality, we have caused and allowed the devastating destruction of our planet. We have stripped Earth of most of its natural beauty and severely polluted much of its land and water. The accumulated effects of our misplaced actions over the last one hundred years have transformed the planet into a wasteland of its former self. There is a direct correlation between our actions and linking the newest mass extinction of species occurring right now on Earth.

Typically, mass extinctions occur from large space impacts or dramatic climate shifts, but in this case, we ourselves are the direct cause. Human beings are now responsible for the loss of more than 50% of all mammal and reptile species on the planet. Most of these organisms survived for millions of years, through apocalyptic scenarios, but in the end, the destructive force of humanity's confusion was too overwhelming for even them. These incredible species have been systematically exterminated because of humanity's blind quest for resources and disconnection to the Earth. In most cases, these special forms of life are gone forever and will exist in nothing more than drawings or photographs. To those unlucky many that may not be important enough to even get this royal treatment, their memory is truly lost in time and forgotten. It's time for mankind to wake up from its long slumber and once again see the spectacular world we call home that is being stolen from all around us as we sleep. I think we have all slept long enough.

This disrespect and suppressed lack of understanding has led humanity into a mad race for acquiring resources as quickly as possible, with no thought about the future. The land masses of the planet have been segregated off into countries with artificial boundaries, where a deep ideology for nationalism was created within society. Human beings have been tricked into believing that a simple birthright gives all merit to an elitism attitude and violence aimed at other nations. The fostering of such intense nationalism has blinded billions of people into the complete hatred of others because of where they were born. This deeply rooted nationalism has fiercely segregated society into nothing more than a group of modern nomadic tribes. This continuous competition against one another has prevented nearly all collaboration of new ideas and slowed down the entire expansion of humanity. These clever distractions to our progression are finally beginning to collapse beneath an ever increasing technologically connected world.

This concept of nationalism that has been stoked in our society for thousands of years has led to hatred, gluttony, severe poverty, and instability across the planet. This structure is reinforced by the intense promotion of competition which begins when we are only children. Whether it is with sports, business, or even societal status, humanity is engineered into a constant state of survival against one another. Instead of a friendly collaboration of ideas with peers, students are pitted against one another in a barbaric matchup for domination. This model for society creates a population who is dominated by ego and greed for themselves. This toxic viewpoint has turned social interactions into a ceaseless barrage of insults and attacks, as we continuously compete for everything.

There has been a deliberate suppression of consciousness for all developed countries and instability and war in virtually all the rest. Not all of this can be blamed on our simple barbarism and left-over cave man tendencies. This may seem like yet another crazy conspiracy theory, but the evidence behind this information speaks volumes. Once again when considering these words, become an objective observer who is peering in from outside. The stubborn stigma that is trained so well into the human psyche regarding this information has left us in a permanent state of laughter and denial whenever the subject is brought up. That is the key to all of this, by becoming an observer of our timeline with a completely unbiased viewpoint and no stigma from the past to govern it. If you are not able to separate yourself from absolute rational thinking, it will be difficult to take in the overall scope of the control that we are under.

Humanity is living in a giant controlled farm with specific sets of rules put in place to distract us and prevent our awareness of knowing the Truth. Most human beings spend the majority of their lives working and have become so accustomed to this ideology of existence that they have become miserable with boredom during their free time. The very phrase 'free time' implies the subtle Truth behind the fact that we are actually slaves on this planet. The title, The Illusion of Us, describes the clever means for our own created reality. Because history dictates for us what reality should be, we simply aren't aware of the Truths behind what freedom and peace can be.

The majority of the human race works for most of their biologically healthiest years, and once they become nonproductive, they are finally free to spend the last remaining moments of their life in a state of sickness and confusion. If we don't work, an individual can lose everything in their life and can even die from starvation if they are not able to earn enough money. The idea that we are living in a modern society that takes care of its citizens is as much as an illusion as everything in reality itself. We believe that the government cares about our well-being and growth, yet they poison the very food and water that is so essential to our health. There is an important need to maintain order and stability across a growingly aware society. So many of the methods for the suppression of human consciousness are hiding right in plain sight, but cannot be seen by an unaware, sleeping population.

The easiest way to keep a population in order in this farm is by promoting and allowing those individuals who follow the rules and do what they are told the best rewards and greatest success. This game of conformity begins when we are very young and often robs us of much of our full childhood experience. If you conform and act normal, you quickly realize that you get into trouble less and receive more rewards. So naturally, many embrace exactly whatever rules are made and do not question anything. Why risk all you have worked for in your life? Propaganda stories bombard children's minds describing the consequences for veering off from this designated model for society and the results to their future. This clever scare tactic deters any child who considers venturing outside the walls of conformity. If we chose to not conform, we often disappoint our parents and are made to feel like a failure. That lack of moral support for being different is one of the main reasons why so many individuals who have more expansive minds end up with a lack of confidence and self-worth. The long road that must be taken in order to remain different and unique is usually a sad and lonely place for most. So many choose to simply give in and conform and forget about who they really are. But no matter what happens, that spark of uniqueness and wonder, processed by so many of these gifted minds will simply lie dormant and wait for a time when it can be accepted and embraced.

Some of us have refused to conform to this model of society and consciously reject their influences. Throughout their younger years, many of these individuals were far too busy embracing the wonders of nature to be bothered by such confinement. For these gifted children, their imagination guided them and designed endless adventures around every corner. But even for these dreamers, there was often no escaping the pressures from public school. The pecking order efficiently arranges everyone in their place early and weeds out those who are different. Our education system follows a strict curriculum for what teachers can and need to teach in public school. If a teacher wants to contribute new lessons into a class, which are outside the boundaries of the selected topics chosen, they can be fired and even lose their teaching certificate. This creates a system where students are forced to learn a conformed version for reality, to control their developing awareness. If a student receives good grades and conforms, they might be able to attend a decent university and are then allowed to become successful in the game of life.

From the very start, the deck is completely stacked for this narrow perspective of success within society, and most importantly within ourselves. Some of us fall right in line with this model of conformity, receiving straight A's on every assignment and then feed off of the energy of encouragement to become patriotic defenders of the system. Those proud parents parade around with bumper stickers boldly displaying the achievements of their child.

But the real question is what did they learn? Conformity is almost mandatory if you wish to succeed in this social game and fiercely rejects those who don't. John F. Kennedy said, "Conformity is the jailer of freedom and the enemy of growth."

Public school is where society is given a controlled view on what to learn and how to act. In many ways, it can be equated to a military like education system. This new model for education has become an indoctrination of the youth into becoming perfect citizens. It teaches them only the skills and knowledge they need to receive basic jobs and where to fit in within a hierarchy of who is considered important. If you feel your child deserves a better education, then you better have a great deal of money and hope that they have been privileged enough to be born with light skin color. In this modern society ruled through money, fair and equal opportunities for learning take a back seat when it comes to providing a consistent education for all citizens.

We must strongly reevaluate the reasons for why so many children simply cannot concentrate or have any interest in so much of what is being taught. Students become buried with homework, stealing away whatever precious free time they had left. When you look at this from the outside as an observer, you wonder when a child developing is ever able to have their own thoughts. They have been robbed of fully experiencing the connections of Mother Nature and their most vital resource of all, time. How many of the classes taught in school connect us to the Earth or the stars above our heads and challenge us to think outside a tightly scripted view of reality? The modern-day education system has been designed to create an ignorant average worker, who is unaware of the Truths of reality. By controlling our education, they control the information that leads to our growth and comprehension later in life.

Consider the different individuals in school who become friends and later stick together in groups to avoid being alone during these difficult development years. In our society, these groups have been broken out and categorized for us based on status. It can be seen plastered through our movies, media, and is sub-consciously trained into our psyche itself. These segregated people receive nearly lifetime labels simply because they are smart or different. Based on that segregation from other children, these social groups are usually cast out from popularity and constantly ridiculed.

Thrown away like garbage, these unique individuals are the keys to our very success in the future. The guards that keep this pecking order in place use bullying to fuel their egos, derived from the very system that created them. This hierarchy structure infused into all of society governs how we think we should act and where we belong. This system heavily favors the more conformed crowd and separates out those who are different into a life of misery and loneliness in the hopes that they will someday just give up and finally conform.

Later on in life, those children who constantly day dreamed and refused to settle for conformity will become the very same ones who will provide breakthroughs to innovation and technology. These special individuals are the keys to humanity's future as they have the gift of imagination and the ability to create. Despite this, society measures success only through those who become wealthy or famous, and this false ideology is believed by the masses who pride themselves on generic jobs and the illusion of happiness in a stiflingly boring existence. No such deviation from this model is considered normal or accepted by anyone. Even those who live in nice neighborhoods are immediately strange and suspect if they do not conform perfectly to the rules. This conditioned fear and ridicule for those who are different, which has imbedded itself deep into the psyche of society, protects the very stability of the system itself, which manifests this illusion through its own desperate need to survive.

Our growing insecurity of one another has turned whole communities into scared strangers, hiding behind endless no trespassing signs. Years of fear propaganda have altered the entire structure of neighborhoods to where children rarely play outside any longer. This disruption of vital childhood development will alter the growth of society for generations to come. We must question the true motivation behind our children's exponential increase in safety, which is wrapped in the clever mirage of compassion. Parents that have succumbed to fear propaganda are under the illusion that their child is safer locked inside, while unknowingly stealing so much of their needed growth, while they pig away on junk food and get little exercise. These fear tactics ripple through every fabric of society and help to falsely define reality for us.

THE ILLUSION OF US

You quickly realize that there is a game very much in place to create a generic society who follows all rules. It favors those who play it correctly and continuously challenges and pushes aside those who do not. Like disciplined soldiers in an army, the population is kept orderly and in its place. The most loyal group in this control system are those who are under the false impression that they have achieved great success by following its rules and fiercely defend its survival. They derive this logic through the over dominance of the human ego, manifested through years of conditioning to create bullies who protect the suppression for all of society. These overly patriotic individuals will verbally or even physically attack another human who differs from the derived viewpoint. Even more outrageous is the fact that they forcefully defend a system of control that enslaves their mind with fear, but offers them nothing real in return but a life of sadness. Reality is built out of the collective mindsets from the past, so through controlling incoming information, everything in the future can be engineered towards a planned outcome.

The true definition of our slavery does not merely lie in the control of our freedoms and thoughts, but through physical labor as well. We are brainwashed into believing we should work as many hours as possible and then come home and waste our free time staring at an electronic box, projecting mindless shows and propaganda. The portrayal of men promoted throughout our culture constantly features them working long hours and then returning home to indulge in free time as long as they watch a barbaric sport on television, which strongly encourages violence and strong masculine strength. On the other side, women in society are expected to fall in line with predetermined gender roles, promoting constant childbearing and widespread ignorance as being their purpose for existence. We must tear down these antiquated gender roles still ruling humanity and allow the freedom of the individual to dictate their future.

Everything in our society is dominated by how we think we should be acting to fit in with one another. Working a job for the majority of our life and then being tied down by mortgages, bills, and even in some cases a family, there leaves little room to find out who we really are as an individual. The most important commodity we have is time and that has been nearly stolen from us. Once a person can finally retire, old and sick from being systematically poisoned and overworked, most of their lives are already over. This human life we have is so precious that we absolutely must not waste it. Our very existence should be viewed as the ultimate gift and cherished for every second that we are able to have our eyes open, and the ability for our lungs to take their next breath.

We are being lied to about our history and who we are, so naturally one must question the interests in us realizing that lie. A lie so big that it would change every fabric of society. Most religions would crumble and anarchy would tear us apart if the Truth got out too quickly. The following information must be taken in strides and not met with anger, but understanding.

There exists a vastly sophisticated control system that has been created to keep people unaware and in a state of order. This system encompasses nearly every part of our life and is the foundation for what creates The Illusion of Us. The complexity found within the system that governs our suppression is almost impossible to consider unless you can comprehend all the pieces involved. It controls every part of both science and religion which forms the foundations for the public's reality. Once you begin to objectively understand each aspect of this control system you will truly be free from it. The thick barriers that protect such loyal nationalism among so much of society will come crumbling down once they begin to embrace this Truth.

The most powerful aspect of the control system is governed through the mainstream religions of the world. Since religion formed the oldest foundations of Truth in our distant past, it became the most insidious of all of these control systems, for its very purpose was to assist in our own awareness and growth of spirituality. As far back as the Roman Empire, the Christian church's use of war and killing in the name of their god has been a disastrous genocide on the human race. What was a message given to us from the great teachings of our ancient elders was re-written and turned into a form of sacrificial idol worship by Marduk (Amun-Ra) and Enlil (Jehovah). This altered model for religion does not promote outside thinking and limits the viewpoint of the person to that of the church. This form of worship feeds off of humanity's deep need for seeking direction in this seemingly hostile existence.

The path towards discovering Truth in ourselves and understanding our place in the universe is only found by fusing the ancient core properties of religion and spirituality, with modern quantum physics. Only through this collaboration can explanations be found for our greatest questions. By separating and controlling both religion and science, "The Illusion of Us" was able to firmly take hold of our reality. Generation upon generation these values and misinformation were carried down to our children and became the base of reality. We must break this cycle once and for all and only provide information that enhances awareness.

The spectacular discovery of the Nag Hammadi Library in Egypt gives us compelling evidence to show a completely different version of the hermetic writings which later became the Bible and provides further proof behind the Archon control system of hijacked religion. The Gnostic people, including the Druids, provided a far more expansive view of the Truth behind our history which was built off of many of the core values of the ancient past such as sacred geometry, which are still revered today on the highest level by modern religion and Freemasonry. These ancient Gnostic writings speak of our deep connection with the stars and the important influences humans have had from the gods and those they called the 'Archons'. These lost writings contain entire chapters that have been removed from the Bible, such as the "Hypostasis of the Archons", which has censored off our awareness of history. Why would all of this important information be suppressed and kept from us?

The head of the Christian church, led by the mighty eagle and Red Cross, ordered their armies to systematically seek out and destroy all ancient Pagan libraries of the past which linked to this forgotten version of the Bible. The Gnostic writings represent the oldest pre-Christian texts ever found and are the most significant evidence we have for how the great teachings of the Bible were meant to be written all along. The concepts found within the ancient roots of religion itself prove that it was meant to be a far different aspect of human growth and followed a spiritual respect for the Earth. Religion was intended to be a celebration of love and our deep spiritual connections to all of life. These ancient teachings were about discovering our divine higher conscious self and understanding our unique connection to the interconnected network which flows through everything in the universe. Once they were able to pollute and control these religious, all of our growth through conscious expansion was severed from us.

While a concerted effort was underway to standardize religions under a central platform of control, a few of the more ancient religions from India and the Himalayan regions adamantly refused this hostile takeover and instead choose to honor their traditional core spiritual beliefs. Some good examples of this lost, pure form of religion can still be found with the practice of Hinduism and Buddhism today. It is by no means a coincidence then that these religions worshiped the snake considering how important and symbolic this reference was to the Enki side of the family. One of the most important writings we have leading back to the truth of who we really are and our deep spiritual side is known as the Nag Hammadi Library, which includes the Nag Hammadi Scriptures and Gnostic Gospels. The word "Nag" or "Naga" translates to mean "snake", showing the ancient connection back to this important symbology of the gods.

The promoted religions, which are still increasing in popularity, enslave their followers into a selectively chosen mindset that discourages individual ideas and creative thinking. The Christian and Catholic churches are the largest proprietors of this false ideology and have caused insurmountable damage to the progression of the human species. What we are taught in school are saints and heroes are often really soldiers of the church cleansing a region from those who differ in mindset or that contain great resources. Examples of this can be found with Columbus, Cortes, and Pizarro who pillaged and stole the resources from the native people of the America's to bolster the Spanish Empire who was controlled by the god of war Ninurta, under the symbol of the Byzantine Eagle. This common theme of conquering native cultures who worship the knowledge of the snake and dragon can be found all across the world and speaks to a hidden war being fought between the dualistic gods of ancient history which continues to this day.

The Christian and Catholic church were transformed into a fierce form of control by Amun-Ra and Enlil and became a conduit for intense violence against any non-believers. This can be seen clearly with the popular religious and cultural celebration known as Saint Patrick's Day, which is celebrated with large amounts of alcohol and green leprechaun's, all of which is used as a distraction from the real Truth of what is actually being celebrated. Saint Patrick was ordered by the church to rid Ireland of all of the "snakes" found there, which was a metaphor for Pagans and Druids since no snakes have ever lived in Ireland, as it is too cold to support them. Saint Patrick, along with his army of the church, murdered and cleansed the remaining Pagans and Druids from Ireland. Ireland and Scotland had become one of the last strongholds of this ancient connection back to the old religion, who's members had built spectacular megalithic monuments such as Stonehenge which aligned with specific star constellations, along with the spring and fall equinoxes. The goal of the church was to destroy all evidence linking the knowledge of the snake and dragon back to Enki and Thoth and to demonize its true meaning. That's why members of the old religion were called "snakes" by the church and can be traced as far back as Adam and Eve with the serpent. The Truth of history is often hidden beneath layers of lies and deception.

The new religions were centrally located under the autocratic arm of the Vatican state, led by the Rothschild family, who assumed total authority for controlling the millions of followers they indoctrinated. Under the influences of the powerfully symbolic Red Cross, the church formed elite death squads made up of its most loyal subjects whose function was to cleanse the population of all pagan followers and destroy any evidence linking the past. This satanic worship of the occult resulted in the deaths of millions of people throughout history. The agenda behind the control of religions was to enslave the population into a selected mindset where their spirituality could be poisoned and used for their own oppression.

The ultimate purpose behind the domination of religions within humanity can be discovered by searching through the ancient records of the past to discover the true secrets behind their intentions. Besides the control of our psyche, the real motive all along has been for the reclaiming of the Holy land by the ancient families. This sacred ground, worth sacrificing so many lives over, is located in the most war-ravaged area on the planet. This ancient cradle of humanity has been devastated by warfare and turned into a literal Hell on Earth. Following the deadly conflicts that revolve around what is now Iraq, Syria, Iran, and Israel, it can be clearly seen that the archaic crusade to take back the sacrificial Holy land has never actually ended. The only thing that has changed over time are the faulty reasons given for military occupation and the continued suffering inflicted on its people for so long.

In the end, all of this makes complete sense if you consider where the scapegoats for hate and orchestrated terrorism have originated from. If society is made to believe that they hate another ethnic group, they will continue to support war there, even at the cost of thousands of innocent people's lives who are merely trying to survive in the conflict-torn nations we have created for them. Most of society can barely even comprehend the scope of violence that has been inflicted to entire generations of people in these regions, whose selfish suffering will echo in the pages of humanity's untold story. I leave you with a quote from Martin Luther King, Jr. that speaks volumes to our current situation here. "An individual has not started living until he can rise above the narrow confines of his individualistic concerns to the broader concerns of all humanity."

One of the greatest secrets that has been kept from society is the Truth behind the properties of two simple colors and what they really represent. All throughout history and peppered through religion and culture, the use of unique color symbology has described a long-fought war over the very future of consciousness in humanity. Two seemingly simple colors describe the internal struggle being fought between the left and right side of the human brain and how we define reality. Along with our own deep mental conflict, the same unique color symbology can be used to describe the underlying struggle for the very future of the planet itself. Will humans on Earth exist in a draconian society, dominated by war and the accumulation of resources, or that of an informative, peaceful society, where humanity can propel itself to the next stage of its own evolution? The decisions that we make in recognizing and following these frequency paths will ultimately determine how our future will play out.

One of the most fundamentally important aspects of understanding the overall methods for how human consciousness and health has been suppressed is through the unique frequencies that the colors of red and blue possess. The reason these particular colors are chosen and worshiped by so many ancient cultures is directly related to the unique states of conscious awareness for which a person can function within them. Our ability to perceive true reality is ultimately dependent by which vibrational frequency we are dominated by. After you read this you will never look at the colors of red and blue the same way again.

The use of precise color symbology directly relates to the underlying fabric of reality itself. If scientists break down human beings to their most basic form, all that remains would be atoms existing in various states of frequency and vibration. What that means is that human beings function like super batteries of energy which feed off of electrical currents. The particular vibrational frequency that a person exists in; represented through their specific state of energy, dictates everything in their reality. Instead of our given name at birth which we distinguish ourselves by, the real identity of the individual should be based on their unique energy signature. I would like to strongly point out that because of the fact that human beings are designed to function in a certain state of high vibrational energy, if a population is kept in a constant state of war, fear, and low vibration, it would essentially represent a type of energy prison for them.

Similar to a fingerprint, each person has their own personal vibrational frequency and when similar frequencies interact, the result is almost always positive. The same came be said about the opposite interaction. That's why most people really do not like being around certain individuals that bring their mood down since they could seek the company of others who make them feel happy. This is not something taught in school, or even really known to most of society. When a person is labeled as having a high metabolism or being overactive, that personality trait translates into a high vibratory rate and frequency. The higher the vibration someone can achieve, the healthier they will be and have the greatest chances for success within they own conscious expansion. This deliberate lowering of human frequency and vibration impacts us on profound levels and suppresses the evolution of our consciousness.

When a human being is kept both mentally and physically in a low vibrational frequency, it means that their consciousness and energy is functioning in the lowest possible state that it can. That's why the root chakra is shown as the color red, matching the specific frequency of visible light spectrum and a slow vibration. By conditioning people to exist primarily in their root chakra and a low state of energy, society has become highly complacent and prone to fear and stress, which greatly limits their capacity to absorb and comprehend complex information. The human body, together with the mind, function poorly in a low state of energy, which is represented as a red-vibrational frequency. This prison of our higher energy greatly limits our potential. A good comparison for this analogy can be found with modern day reptile's and mammals. Picture yourself observing a group of turtles sunning themselves on a warm log, or a group of alligators clinging together for warmth in a zoo. These creatures which are found within the reptile family and must constantly seek a warm internal temperature in order conserve their energy consumption. Because the reptile must function in a slower frequency and vibration than that of mammals, they exist in a red-vibrational spectrum of existence. Mammals, on the other hand, exist on the opposite side of the spectrum from red, even if we have developed a collective amnesia to that Truth.

Despite the fact that human beings are mammals, the left side of the brain is still dominated by the ancient lineage back to reptiles and a purely analytical mindset with a lack of compassion. By allowing the masculine or left side of the brain to control our governing and identity, the barbaric and senseless domination of society through warfare has disconnected humanity from itself and the planet. Through understanding these two sides of the brain and how certain vibrational frequencies factors into our conscious and energetic state, the path that humanity has taken becomes much more clear. The most useful way to interpret and rationalize these two lobes of the brain and how consciousness functions within them is by explaining the relative vibrational frequency to which the colors of red and blue are perceived through. Picture a friendly afternoon soccer game in which two teams need to be chosen. They take to the field, wearing the colors of red and blue and race towards the ball. Without knowing it, they have taken part in the universal struggle I like to call red verse blue.

Since the state of our awareness is directly dependent on these color frequencies and wavelengths, the seemingly unknown battle taking place all around us represents our very future here. In the United States, the control of the political process is fought over between the red elephants and blue donkeys. Both of these lobes of governing can be directly equated to represent the left and right side of the human brain as well as the ancient family factions of the Anunnaki. The Republicans pride themselves on military force and the domination of wealth for their country, while on the other side, the Democrats claim to seek peace and a general compassion for humanity. In reality, both of these parties have largely become irrelevant and are simply false sides of the same corrupt and broken system, controlled by elite bankers at the top of the pyramid. True democracy was lost in the United States when President Kennedy was assassinated by the CIA when he tried to gain control of its monetary systems. This great vision of freedom, being progressively eroded, was laid down by the founding fathers and can be seen clearly with the Washington Memorial, which is actually an Egyptian obelisk.

The colors of red and blue dominate our subconscious perception and examples for their use can still be found all over the world. Red and blue are also the most commonly used colors for the representation of country flags and in many military uniforms. With so many striking correlations found everywhere for the use of red and blue, we must stop and strongly consider the deeper reasons behind them, and if there isn't truly more to this story than what meets the eye. The battle over simple colors may seem trivial to many at first until they fully understand the properties of what they represent for our consciousness. In popular culture throughout history, those individuals whose clothing or faction represented the color blue were consistently considered the "good" guys, while those representing by red are always the "bad" guys. This logic has defined itself within all of society without giving anyone a basis as to why. The answer to that question opens the doorway to understanding the long forgotten ancient struggle of our past and future.

Blue and red exist at nearly opposite ends of the visible light spectrum. They are about as different as colors can be. Even more interesting is that blue light has a cooler temperature than red light. I find it fascinating that colors can have these properties and yet little of this knowledge is taught to society. Blue is also considered to be the favorite color for the majority of all people on Earth. Imagine the temperature of a cold alpine lake, compared to a volcano spewing out searing hot lava. The colors that are represented follow the wavelength for what the elements are. The human body is made up primarily out of water. We are like super-conductors of energy that have electricity flowing through our charged system.

Since we are mammals and our genetic make-up is dominated by water, our matching wavelength represents blue and a cooler temperature. The blue wavelength also represents a much higher energetic state of matter which you can see clearly with a comparison of both on a chart. If wavelength determines our physical state then frequency determines our mental one. The human skeleton, along with the specific frequency that the brain tunes into will determine what kind of antenna it functions as. Each frequency, similar to the wavelengths of visible light, follows a specific pattern for optimal functioning. That means that a person's brainwave state and physical state, following the frequencies of red and blue, will determine everything in their reality. If we look at the chakra system in the human body we see that it matches up precisely to the colors of the visible light spectrum. No matter what, if a person remains in their root chakra and the matching frequency of the color red, they will be severely limited in the growth of their higher consciousness. Our ability to correctly understand reality is based on our mental and physical condition.

We should re-examine how this information fits into our overall perceptions of history and the collective consciousness on Earth. If we understand the laws behind visible light we will conquer most boundaries in our way. Realize that the red wavelength of light is long and slow and represents a much warmer state of matter. Think of a large overweight person, spending their time sitting on a couch and getting very little exercise. That person exists in a red vibrational frequency that controls their ability to perceive reality and poisons their mind.

It is very interesting to me that in the movie the "Matrix," Neo is given the choice of "waking up" by taking a pill represented through the use of red and blue. With all the Truth given in this movie, it is quite shocking to see that when it comes to the importance of this very color choice that they have deliberately decided to trick the audience for those not being objective. Blue would always represent the choice of human beings waking up since it matches our higher chakra centers. The Truth behind these colors represents an invisible world of frequencies and wavelengths battling one another for domination. But beyond the linear view that this is simply just a movie, the questions Neo is asked and the important decisions he must make portray the very future of humanity itself. In the represented reality we live in, most of society would quickly choose the red pill and decide to stay asleep for the rest of their lives in a state of ignorance. It is those who are brave enough to choose the blue pill and awaken to the Truths of reality that I speak to now. This conscious choice we must make internally is almost unknown to everyone in society. Without even realizing it, we have allowed this sickness of our mind to take over everything that governs our lives and controls our reality.

This red and blue world we exist in directly translates into information or lack of information. Because the human brain is broken up into two distinct lobes, known as the left and right brain, considerable effort has been orchestrated upon society in order to promote the prominence of the left side. Since the left brain represents the ancient reptilian side and the right brain, the mammal side, the underlying agenda all along has been for the total dominance of the left or red side in humanity. It is by no means a coincidence then that the elite controlling family in charge of society known as 'Rothschild', literally translates to mean 'red shield'. It can be clearly seen after looking over all of the evidence that these elite families suppressing consciousness have been the defenders of the red frequency all along. These battling frequencies found within us ultimately derive from a lack of collaboration together.

Only by the unification of both of these sides can one achieve balance and the expansion of their consciousness. This struggle of the two sides of the human brain fighting over one another has been written about and shown in countless symbols for thousands of years. Once you understand this essential principle, you begin to see it all around you, from movies and television to books and creative designs. For thousands of years these symbolic teachings that describe the hidden struggle of dark verse light, and red verse blue, have woven themselves into so much of our culture and society. They can be found all around us and almost scream out to be seen and connected. These lessons that have been carried down from multitudes of ancient cultures all strive for us to simply understand ourselves. What looks like a battle is actually meant to be a collaboration all along.

Instead of the concepts of "evil" red fighting against "good" blue, it must be realized that in order to achieve this beautiful spectrum of color which makes up the foundations for all of light, there must be unification between all of them. When you break all of this down to its simplest level, it is all just light and the absence of that light which describes the entire universe. The same struggle playing out all around us in the cosmos is the very same one we are battling within ourselves. It is the necessary conflict in order to create a perfect duality for learning. In the future when this knowledge is truly understood and accepted by society, we will have reached peace both physically and mentally. This critical test that measures our own development as a species is the key to insuring our own evolution and the mutual survival of humanity.

There are many ways that the suppression of knowledge can delay our expansion, but the controlling of new technology is one of the most influential methods. Technology may seem like it is moving at light speed, but the unbiased reality is that society is comparably still living in the stone-age. Since the early 1950's, there has been a cap on inventions and patents that would have led to great breakthroughs in technology. Most of these technologies revolve around frequency, energy, and even gravity. Famous inventors like Nikola Tesla and Henry Moray would have changed the very world as we know it until their work was destroyed and Truth suppressed. Throughout the last 60 years, inventors have come up with ways to rid us of fossil fuels and change the very face of energy use itself. Many of those who have tried to disclose this information and the corruption behind it, have turned up floating in a river, or conveniently considered a "suicide". All connections to this information are lost and many who try and speak out are threatened, along with their families. There is a lot at stake in keeping these new technologies secret from the public. Much of what we know is due to the sacrifices these brave whistleblowers have made to expose the Truth.

The electronic devices that we use every day are considered safe and essential to our existence. Television sets, phones, and most electronics emit a slow red frequency, which negatively affects any person around them. I cannot emphasize the importance of these color frequencies enough and what they represent to the functionality of a human. The invisible frequencies that emanate from so many of the devices that we use daily have been engineered as a powerful tool to keep our frequency locked into a red wavelength form. The average person now spends far more time watching television than even going outside and this shift is portrayed as completely normal in society. This dramatic cultural change has poisoned our mindsets and severed our connection with Mother Nature. By designing these electronic devices to emit a slow red frequency, a powerful form of mind control is used to enslave the entire population. Since a human beings ability to absorb information is directly related to its state of frequency, this ancient battle over red and blue will be the ultimate deciding factor for the future. Will humanity choose to exist in a world dominated by a red frequency and succumb to the inevitable destruction of their species, or will they instead fight back to regain all that has been stolen from their blue past?

Television has the ability to connect us with useful information and to the world, but it's used far less for that purpose anymore. The main function of this modern television set has become a powerful tool for spreading propaganda through the use of mind control. Since all of the major television networks are owned by the same large media corporations, which are ultimately managed by the elite families, an agenda is followed for the regulation and manipulation of nearly all television programs. Everything from the news to commercials is controlled by this secret hand of the elites who propel a certain agenda. Since television has been the dominant means of information and news for generations, it is easy to see how quickly people became shells of fear and misinformation. Terence McKenna brilliantly said, "Television is by nature the dominator drug par excellence. Control of content, uniformity of content, repeatability of content, makes it inevitably a tool of coercion, brainwashing, and manipulation."

The large media companies that control society through clever programming and frequency are one of the greatest means for suppressing consciousness. They are the mouthpiece for informing society to what is real and what we think we should like. Society watches reality shows about other people's excessively frivolous lives and tries to strive for their illusion of success. These shows distract us from the harsh realities we exist in and suppress any conscious thought of seeking real happiness. If an individual tries to start an expansive discussion relating around consciousness or brings up a taboo topic like extraterrestrial existence, they are usually laughed at and ridiculed by their peers and seen as crazy. Because of this, designated safe topics are instead chosen by the majority of people to remain accepted and normal to others. Those topics that can expose Truth and challenge the oligarchy system controlling us are made into jokes for our amusement which instantly destroy their credibility when brought up. I for one am unbelievably bored with normal.

Our very existence here has become perceived by society as commonplace to simply sail through life as oblivious and ignorant as possible. This form of awareness is promoted heavily in the media and celebrated by the majority of the public. This promotion of a materialistic existence to reality is shown through the use of popular television shows which celebrate a certain lifestyle of carefree spending and constant dining out. Being in debt from credit cards is seen as normal and buying as many material things as possible is highly encouraged. We are told that happiness is only found in the items we can afford to purchase and seek out a constant supply of this illusion to fill the empty void. This lifestyle leads to immense debt and an increased dependency on financial income. Very little happiness is actually found in these material items and more often than not they end up sitting in the back of a dusty garage, forgotten. The most important thing that was stolen from us through this illusion of materialism is time itself, as most people will spend the rest of their lives paying for their mistakes.

In only a few generations, we have seen an almost complete loss and merging of the most powerful media companies together. Now just a handful of large corporate names has managed to completely dominate whatever message they want to get across to the public. This controlling viewpoint is accomplished through heavily influenced political candidates and propaganda. The way that these large corporations, who are owned by the elite families, are able to secure their interest and message is through the manipulation of a corrupt political process.

The elite families in charge of society will choose a predetermined political candidate who is given financial support to run for an important office seat. That candidate is given almost unlimited financial backing in order to successfully become elected. In many cases these candidates are chosen years before and put through intense grooming, much like a prized poodle in a dog show would receive. These groomed candidates are taught how to speak charismatically to the average person and to invoke trust, even if the message itself is wrong. Instead of a candidate running with new ideas and compassion for the future, the political process has become a game, designed around those who are the most attractive and well spoken. The substance of their message has been conditioned into most people to simply not matter any longer. This dog and pony show is starting to finally break down and become exposed for what it really is. The revolution that has taken hold of politics across the globe is merely the outcry of awareness building across so much of humanity.

The largest corporations in the world, made up by the four most powerful banks and energy companies, control nearly every government across the planet and the billions of people that reside there. With the elite family hierarchy controlling above them, the model for wealth distribution became a complete trickle-down effect, with very little being received by the average person while the vast majority is funneling straight to the top. This pyramid of wealth redistribution has left millions of people across the planet sick and hungry while a lucky few live in gluttony. The wealthier societies found within the most dominant countries over world affairs became consciously poisoned through their promoted obsession with nationalism and material gain. This has led to both obesity epidemic's and food shortages occurring at the same time and speaks to a broken system which is unsustainable.

This madness brainwashed into so much of society has polarized our viewpoint, while blindly allowing the theft of crucial resources from the poor and starving nations of the Earth. This domination over the less fortunate is perpetuated through the use of military force and threatening financial intimidation. Martin Luther

King, Jr. once famously said, "We must rapidly begin the shift from a 'thing-oriented' society to a 'person-oriented' society. When machines and computers, profit motives and property rights are considered more important than people, the giant triplets of racism, materialism, and militarism are incapable of being conquered."

The elite families controlling all governments have worked carefully to influence every means of our life and perception. The more you learn about these methods, the more sinister it truly becomes. We must not shy away from information simply because it is hard to hear. If looking at all of this from an objective standpoint, it should become clear that the government is not here to support our best interests, but rather, to sicken our bodies and suppress our consciousness. By remaining ignorant to all of this information, the enslavement of society is allowed to continue and threatens to finally extinguish the spark within our true identity.

The following summary focuses on the extensive ways in which society is targeted in order to suppress their consciousness and maintain order. The designed purpose behind this is to prevent our awareness as long as possible from the Truth of reality and continue the status quo. The very air we breathe, the water we drink, and the food we eat is all integrated into the matrix of conscious suppression that sickness of our bodies and minds. Picture yourself outside on a bright sunny day, without a cloud anywhere in sight. You go inside to have some lunch and by the time you come out the sky is now a mix of long linear and crisscross style clouds, expanding and blocking out the sun. Puzzled, you scratch your head and think back on the forecast which called for a sunny day without a cloud in the sky. You might wonder what happened to the sun for a few moments, but then simply brush it off as nothing as you don't want to cause any unnecessary concern to your subconscious. That increasingly familiar occurrence is known as a chemtrail.

When a large plane flies by overhead, it naturally creates temporary clouds called contrails. Try and separate the two terms, and remember the difference. A contrail is perfectly normal and should dissipate in few seconds, depending on moisture levels in the atmosphere. However, when the contrail continues to grow larger, eventually merging with other similar trails and filters out entire portions of the sky, that is what is known as a chemtrail. A chemtrail is an artificially created cloud that has been seeded and does not dissipate like a normal contrail. This technique of seeding is done by injecting aluminum and lithium into the atmosphere as part of a global geoengineering project. Next time you are outside on a clear day, keep a watchful eye to the sky so that you can see for yourself the Truth in these words. We do not fully understand the degree to which we have been poisoned and controlled because of the ultimate secrecy revolving around this material.

Public drinking water is another major target for the suppression of awareness in society. This unsettling tactic has been used as a primary means for sickening the public and suppressing consciousness for more than 40 years. Fluoride in various amounts is dumped into our public drinking supplies for 70% of water in the United States. Other similar ratios exist in most developed countries around the world. Health experts boast that it helps strengthen teeth enamel and prevent cavities, which is actually true. The problem is that fluoride is completely toxic when consumed. If you think that it is safe, take a look at the back of a toothpaste bottle for what it says if you accidentally ingest it. Fluoride is a poisonous substance to our system and causes detrimental long-term neurological damage. The use of it in public drinking water affects both our neural and biological functions of the body. These effects over time produce a population with a reduced IQ and a disruption to critical components of the brain. Drinking large amounts of natural spring water every day can do profound, positive changes in our body and help to awaken the human mind from its long slumber.

The real underlying purpose behind the addition of Fluoride into public drinking water is not merely to lower our IQ, or even to make us sick. The real reason for the use of Fluoride is to block off a very particular part of the human brain called the pineal gland. This secret and almost unknown gland, located just above the brain stem, has been called the "third eye" by intellects and advanced cultures all throughout history. This sacred component of the brain is the gateway to knowledge and Truth behind the expansion of human consciousness. The pineal gland plays an integral role in the very evolution of humanity. It is no coincidence that this special gland is almost unheard of in society and is rarely studied or taught when learning about the human brain. Activation of the pineal gland allows a rapid shift in the perception of information and Truth. Fluoride, and other neural toxins block off and crystalize this gland, rendering it completely useless until activated. There it remains, dormant, until a time when society is permitted the total freedom of thought and information. You can learn much more about how to activate your pineal gland in the expansion chapter.

The very foods we buy are treated with unhealthy chemical pesticides or injected with artificial growth hormones, which are then consumed by the population and leached into our bodies. The combined effect from these pollutants in the body can lead to generations of disease and sickness. Home cooked meals prepared with fresh ingredients have become a thing of the past and have been replaced by Tran's fat-rich fast foods instead. The fatty, high sodium rich meals we consume almost daily that are constantly bombarded to us through clever advertising are highly unhealthy and damaging to our system. These unhealthy foods, along with pesticides and the various hormones accumulated within them, have not only caused countless deaths but the suppression for so much of what could have been for humanity.

The average person now rarely consumes food from a locally grown organic farm and instead relies on food trucked from across thousands of miles away, from giant government subsidized farms. That is how so much of our food is able to be delivered to us in this contaminated state. With the federally run Food and Drug Administration merely eating out of the hands of billionaires, these atrocities were allowed to be perpetrated on the unknowing population. The outcome to society from so many years of tainted consumption has led to disease and obesity cases shooting through the roof. This polluting of our bodies lowers human vibration and sickens the mind, allowing it to function in a state of almost insanity.

The illusion of our accomplishments has given people the false impression that they deserve to be served food almost daily by a restaurant or through fast food. The barrage of commercials and television shows we watch idealizes this standard of carefree living and ignores the need for financial planning and saving. Most of the meals found in restaurants and fast food establishments are loaded with artificial ingredients and colors that greatly contribute towards the continued sickening of our bodies. So much of our suppression can be linked directly back to the disappearance of healthy, home cooked meals. Instead of eating organically grown fresh fruits, vegetables, and lean protein, we clog our bodies with foods specifically engineered to taste as good as possible. Human beings are like organic computers that are full of viruses which keep our conscious state bogged down in complete ignorance of the Truth.

The United States has witnessed a dramatic increase in cases of autism, which has directly coincided with the increased distribution of childhood vaccinations. The concept of protecting a child from disease is completely logical and necessary in many cases. However, the issue resides in exactly what is being put into these vaccinations, as well as the large doses given at such a young age. When a child is young and still at a crucial development stage in their life, an overload of vaccinations given over a very short period of time can dramatically weaken the immune system of the individual. Alongside the unsettling increases with autism, there has also been a dramatic rise in neurological diseases as well. Correlation must be seen in regards to the implementation of widespread vaccination use and the explosion of these degenerate diseases.

Neurological diseases such as multiple sclerosis and epilepsy, which used to be rare and almost unheard of, have exploded in our society. Many of the rapid rises seen in disease coincide with the increased implementation of these vaccinations in our children due to the toxic heavy metals present. We must take a hard look at what goes into the developing human child and how best to protect their health and future. We as free people need to stand up and question our health and the medicine being put into our bodies. The notion that our governments care about the health and well-being of its citizens should be strongly reexamined. No longer will we blindly take whatever is given to us without first doing our own research. It is the right of every human being to be firmly in charge of their own health and mind.

The word medicine means to cure or heal, but in a broader sense, it should be that which is safe and beneficial for the human body and mind. We have lost our way because of the influences of money and the need to dumb down consciousness. The word medicine can no longer be used in the context of those sanctioned drugs that are given to us. In the United States, new pharmaceutical drugs are advertised through a barrage of commercials on television, in magazines, and giant bill boards. The commercials promise a happy life and a way to take away all the pain from this reality. As human beings become more aware of their individual self, they begin to realize their unhappiness and seek for ways to cure it. These pharmaceutical drugs provide a temporary solution for that emptiness that come with the side effects of severe addiction and damage to vital organs over time. The illusion of modern medicine lies within its artificial components. By brainwashing society into believing that these chemicals are beneficial, they have systematically sickened and addicted millions of people which will affect entire generations to come.

Most of the drugs that are allowed in society like tobacco and alcohol are promoted everywhere and celebrated. These substances poison our bodies and suppress our consciousness and yet they are cheered on by a sick population that cannot see the true harm. A celebration of any kind automatically means alcohol is needed, and a stressful situation is frequently coddled by cigarettes. Those drugs that bring benefit to society are allowed and even heavily promoted, while those that expand the mind are banned and highly illegal. These sanctioned drugs can be easily purchased on nearly every corner in a community and feed into enhancing poverty stricken regions and the struggling people within them. A direct correlation can be seen by which communities have the highest density of liquor stores and those with the highest crime and illiteracy rates. This non-coincidental connection, along with the war on drugs, creates countless, broken communities who are segregated off from the rest of society. This model highly benefits a government which worries about supporting an old population through social security programs and targets areas of certain ethnicities that are deemed undesirable.

In most cases, the government itself financially supports and provides massive subsidies to the tobacco and alcohol industry. By promoting the heavy use of tobacco to the public, which results in the deaths of more than a million people a year worldwide, the governments annually perpetrate a quiet genocide of its own citizens. Yet even though we are finally learning the Truth behind these dangerous sanctioned substances, we still ignore the underlying fact that the government is trying to suppress and sicken us. Most people simply laugh at this information and drink their sadness away never asking the necessary questions in the obvious insanity for what our society has become.

The war on drugs has been yet another powerful weapon against the expansion of consciousness. This artificial war has convinced people that simple plants and herbs are dangerous, while others substances that are sanctioned are acceptable and fine. The government accomplished this collective mindset view through propaganda and fear. The basis for this secret war is not about keeping people safe from drugs, but rather to keep certain psychoactive substances highly illegal and challenging to obtain and research. The other function of this drug war was to systematically strip away remaining freedoms. By scaring the public and lying about most of the true facts, there was little objection to using race as a means to search and arrest people. Entire communities have been destroyed by this war, which is nothing more than a means to control what we think and punish those who wander outside mainstream acceptability.

The war on drugs is also responsible for the increasingly profitable and highly incentivized drug testing of our society. This gross overreach of our individual sovereign freedoms has infiltrated much our education system, workplace, and career choices. Drug testing is a draconian attempt at controlling a population, by segregating out those who choose to use certain forbidden substances. The majority of the public assumes these tests are done in order to protect the individual from the dangerous drugs that could harm them. In actuality, it couldn't be further from the Truth. Drug testing is done to "weed out" those who refuse to play the game of conformity and are being punished for their temptations to alter consciousness. Because the artificial substances that are actually harmful like heroin, or cocaine, only stay in the user's system for up to 36 hours, they are rarely ever found during testing. Natural psychedelic substances like cannabis can stay in a person's system for up to a month. This stark difference is due to how these fatty-like, natural compounds can bind with associated receptors and remain in the blood stream.

The true purpose of drug testing is to rid society of people who use conscious expanding substances. That is the real reason for lumping them together with other schedule 1 controlled substances, which also prevents them from being studied. Under the careful mask of compassion, drug testing companies have made billions of dollars by ruining people's lives. What a person does to their consciousness in the privacy of their own home is none of the governments business. This gross overuse of power is starting to slowly fade away as we become aware of this obvious injustice. The society of the future will look back at this time period and mock these laughable attempts at controlling our individual freedoms.

The United States, supposedly founded on freedom and Truth, has by far the highest incarceration rate of its citizens in jail in the world. This amusing oxymoron is anything but funny to the millions of people locked away for simple petty crimes and drug possession. For those lucky few who are finally released from prison, their life is ruined forever because of the black mark on their permanent record. If you consider the murder rates in other countries or even their populations in comparison, nothing justifies this incarceration rate except for control and profit. With a thriving private prison industry, there is incentive for finding ways to lock people away. The sad Truth is that our society is far from being free. It is simply the false promotion of freedom, while still maintaining the status quo of control.

The bloated prison industry, combined with the war on drugs, is responsible for countless families being torn apart and millions of lives ruined. This symbiotic relationship depends on each another and there is great lobbying power behind its continued success. By creating an enormous underground market for drugs, this dark business model directly leads to extensive violence, instability, and a complete disruption of communities. All across the world, the war on drugs has inflicted countless tragedies and death. For countries like Mexico, who developed extensive drug cartels supplying the huge U.S. black market, unimaginable violence has been inflicted there. Over 50,000 innocent Mexican citizens have been murdered by the madness this war has created in the last few years alone. So many people think that the war on drugs helps keep us safe and protected, but the Truth is, it will be looked back on as one of the worst policy disasters in human history.

The largest tragedy from the drug war, beyond the horrible human suffering, is how our entire future of this planet was simply stolen from us. The secret underlying purpose for the war on drugs was actually created to suppress and demonize the Truth about hemp and cannabis. No other plant in human history has had such monumental efforts attempted at eradication and extermination than the cannabis plant. This special plant provides nearly endless renewable resource potential, along with life-saving medical benefits and a powerful means for expanding consciousness. Hemp is simply the non-psychoactive version of the cannabis plant. The confusion behind understanding the Truth about this miraculous weed stems from the total ignorance found within the public over not realizing that there are different sexes and types for the cannabis plant and the important benefits each one provides. Decades of intense propaganda fueled with lies has taken a heavy toll on most people's personal views towards this "plant" within the subconscious. Let us clear the air and only provide Truth without irrational feeling.

Hemp, simply the non-psychoactive male version of cannabis, is the strongest natural fiber in the world. Before it was outlawed, hemp was considered essential to so much of our developing world. Where would we be today without its extensive assistance in our history? All of the sails on boats, flags, paper, clothes, textiles, and so much more was being made with primarily hemp until it was made illegal. Hemp paper, clothes, and textiles could completely replace wood and cotton and last 10 times longer which was seen as a direct threat to men like William Randolph Hearst, who controlled the newspaper and timber industry. If not systematically blocked and made illegal to the public, cannabis and hemp would have represented a completely alternate future for the Earth and society. Instead of traveling down this bright road, we were instead forced down a path dominated by dirty fossil fuels and an economy reliant on those products made from petroleum and plastics. This alternative future, derived from immense greed and corruption, has severely polluted and nearly destroyed the planet's ecosystems. This was achieved through the rampant spreading of false propaganda within the public, where cannabis was demonized and considered the greatest enemy standing in the way of their agenda.

The unfortunate reality that has been forced upon society, consists of an unsustainable economy which is completely dependent on depleting the Earth of ancient fossilized organic matter and the domination of synthetics for its survival. Without understanding the extensive properties of cannabis and the potentials for what it provides, much of this information may seem ridiculous and silly. It will take a considerable amount of time to repair much of this deeply entrenched hate within our subconscious towards many of the Truths in life.

Besides replacing fossil fuels, cotton, and nearly all other industrial products, the greatest value for cannabis lies in the medical properties it contains. The different uses for cannabis greatly depend on which gender is needed for a specific purpose. The male plant gives us food, clothing, and shelter, while the female provides us with wisdom, peace of mind, and health. The impressive ways in which cannabis can improve health is due to the highly protected properties that lie within its natural compounds. These natural compounds uniquely bind with a secret system in our bodies that is not even taught in medical textbooks. This unique internal regulatory system in mammals is called the endocannabinoid system. It regulates everything from mood and appetite, to pain sensation and memory. This is accomplished through receptors found all throughout our body, including in the brain. These receptors are called cannabinoid receptors, which bind with the human body's creation of anandamide, which exactly mirrors cannabinoids produced only by the cannabis plant. This unique plant has a special symbiotic relationship with humans that dates back for thousands of years.

One day this solitary hero will receive the praise and respect it truly deserves. The untold medical breakthroughs possibly through cannabis will revolutionize all of medicine in the future. By hiding all of this information from the public and concealing the Truth behind what seems like just a silly weed, a vital part of our regulatory system can remain hidden from us. All of this carefully falls into the overall scope of suppressing consciousness and health.

As I write this, the important ancient healing plants and fungi found within the family of psychedelics, are still considered a schedule 1 substance and are the most restricted. These restrictions come with devastating consequences if caught by law enforcement and possession can ruin an entire person's future. The reason for this is because psychedelics expand human perception and break free the associated stigmas entrained into our psyche. Terence McKenna said, "Psychedelics are illegal not because a loving government is concerned that you may jump out of a third-story window. Psychedelics are illegal because they dissolve opinion structures and culturally laid down models of behavior and information processing. They open you up to the possibility that everything you know is wrong."

If you look throughout human history at so many of the brilliant breakthroughs, inventions, and great leaps in our progression, most of them can be attributed to psychedelics. They are our natural allies here to aid us in expansion and in the pursuit of Truth. Almost every item listed in the highly restricted schedule 1 status is a natural or artificial psychedelic, except for one obvious substance. It would be too conspicuous if not for the feared substance of heroin being present. Heroin, which is derived from opium, is indeed a very dangerous drug. However what most do not know, is that it is virtually the same compound as Morphine, or Oxycodone, which are frequently prescribed to the public. There are many other opioid-based drugs that are regularly given out by the pharmaceutical industry as part of what we have been made to believe is "medicine".

How could this have happened to medicine? Medicine's ancient purpose was to make us feel better and become healthy. These days you can die from simply misreading the instructions on the back of a commonly available, over-the-counter medication. Modern medicine has become dangerous, synthetically created compounds peddled by drug dealing doctors, unaware of their true consequences. When profit became the motive behind medicine, the incentives behind healing people and finding cures became illusions themselves. On a deeper level, the many medications that suppress so much of our consciousness are heavily encouraged through massive profit gains.

Planet Earth contains everything humanity needs to heal and grow from within nature itself. Since natural substances cannot be patented, there is little interest from modern medicine in their use.

From the ancient cultures still thriving deep in the Amazon rainforest to the spiritual shamans high up in the Himalayan Mountains, humans have always had a connection with the natural medicines from the Earth. This deviation is a large reason for the continued sickness and suppression of consciousness in society. The giant pharmaceutical companies who are pedaling these synthetic based cures for "happiness" have been responsible for countless deaths and suffering. We may never know how many have died from these "medicines," but one day the Truth will be exposed as a black mark for the medical industry.

The most effective technique for the suppression of consciousness is achieved through **fear**. Fear is the most powerful tool for controlling a population and keeping it in a stagnant state of expansion. A human, dominated by fear will exist in the lowest vibrational form of consciousness they can. This tactic is achieved by bombarding society with alarming images that frighten us and make us feel like we need protection for our continued survival. The population is groomed into a state of constant stress and fear and driven towards the hatred of other ethnic groups and religions.

The most vital concept to realize for the success of expanding consciousness is that fear is not real. It is merely a tool for the control of the public and simply a leftover aspect of our ancient left brain. If you do not feed the negative energy of fear itself, it will not exist within you. Fear amplifies stress and locks our consciousness in a left brain mentality for survival. Through the use of fear, humans make nonrational decisions and are easily led down a path of violence. No other method of control in all of human history has led to such profoundly negative consequences to our own expansion and advancement.

Humanity must take a hard look at the precise events leading up to each major human conflict that escalated into a large-scale war. From the First World War to Vietnam, all of these conflicts were carefully created, with humanity being used as nothing more than the conduits of violence for tyrant leaders. With the orchestrated sinking of the Lusitania by its own country, the First World War was romanced by society as a heroic and brave act, with little consideration of the true reality. Droves of young men quickly joined the fight, leaving their families behind in the name of nationalism. Confidently rushing into combat, the romantic illusion of their sacrifice was only made clear to them after thousands came home in coffins.

The most important question we have to ask ourselves is, did so many innocent people have to die at all? The propaganda and fear that has severely influenced society for so long has convinced the public that these acts of violence are necessary and needed. This despicable treatment of humanity will echo on in our memories and will someday be viewed by a future society with embarrassment and heavy sadness. How many millions of people had to die for the lust of the military-industrial complex, or the massive wealth gains from the elite controlling families?

Perpetual warfare has become the dominant feature for much of the Middle Eastern countries, as well as large portions of the African continent. This ancient region of the world has been the target of hate and instability for thousands of years. Even if a nation is not fighting a war on their own soil, they are likely taking part in supporting these deadly conflicts that continue to ravage the lives of millions of people who live there. By scapegoating the Middle East region, specifically the Muslim people, a seemingly creditable outside attacker was created. This alleged attacker, hailing from this war-torn region, was portrayed as hiding in caves and possessing the ability for advanced bomb making and elaborate attacks across the world. The media uses propaganda to further spread fear and give the illusion that radical jihadist could be hiding anywhere and strike at any time.

The orchestration for high-level acts of created terrorism on society, most famously September 11, 2001, are what are known as false flag attacks. These acts of violence carried out in a very public setting are designed to create fear, hate, and patriotic support for the military-industrial complex. All one has to do is look into Operation Northwoods, where the United States practiced drills hijacking commercial planes in order to blame other countries as a means to start a war. Many of the true motives behind going to war are kept secret from the public and are never disclosed. The commonly used tactic by the United States is to create a grand spectacle which is perpetrated in full view of the public, by the use of bombs or a mass shooting. After the event occurs, the public will cry out for immediate action be taken, being driven by overwhelming media coverage that promotes fear and nationalism, without asking the needed questions to get to the real Truth of the matter.

While searching for evidence in the aftermath, the authorities will miraculously find an unscathed pair of passports, which perfectly identify the apparent terrorists. Certain familiarities will immediately reoccur after each event, from the need to increase military spending and support, to an attempt at banning all guns from the public. The controlled mass media uses these events to portray a state of complete anarchy across the world. This clever maneuver is part of the ancient agenda for establishing a military-run society, where all of our remaining freedoms are removed. The implications for this coerced outcome for the future would envision a modern Nazi state under a single world government, and has the uncanny appearance of something right out of the book "1984".

The promotion of instability across the Middle East and other parts of the world, leading to so many devastating conflicts, is the primary tactic used by the powerful military-industrial complex to sustain their continued funding and purpose. In his last speech before leaving office as president, Dwight D. Eisenhower warned the American people, and the world, of the dangers of the military-industrial complex and the control it can have on all of society. When we contemplate on all the things a president prefers to say when they are leaving office, this should stand as a stark reminder to emphasize the seriousness and Truth behind this information. President Eisenhower's final address to the nation included these chilling words: "In the councils of government, we must guard against the acquisition of unwarranted influence, whether sought or unsought, by the military-industrial complex. The potential for the disastrous rise of misplaced power exists and will persist. We must never let the weight of this combination endanger our liberties or democratic processes. We should take nothing for granted. Only an alert and knowledgeable citizenry can compel the proper meshing of the huge industrial and military machinery of defense with our peaceful methods and goals, so that security and liberty may prosper together."

Humanity has been warned repeatedly by past leaders and presidents, some of whom have even lost their lives over revealing some of this important information. But time and time again, we refuse to see the Truth and instead prefer to remain within our own ignorance. War is a means of instability, profit, and total control of a population. I find it fascinating that we call extreme policies that are seemingly inhumane draconian policies, considering the root of the word. It can be easy to let this information depress and anger you but we must simply realize the past and then let go of its fear based grip over us. Always remember that knowledge is power.

It can be very difficult to comprehend so much of this shocking information and believe that it is in fact real. I can assure you that the only purpose for the release of this information is to protect Truth. The most important commodity to humanity is time itself. All of these tactics used to suppress consciousness are simply a delaying of the inevitable awakening and disclosure that will come. By connecting all of this information together, an elaborate framework begins to be emerge showing the sheer scope and magnitude of this overall suppression of consciousness. Behind this dark shadow, we see that the purpose all along was to prevent our realization of who we really are and the gifts locked within our noncoding or "junk" DNA. The most important question we must always ask first is **why**. The why is what always leads to Truth.

As the system begins to flounder and desperately throws all it has at the human race, we must put its negative influences of fear behind us and only look towards the future. In many ways, humanity is like a flock of sheep being led by a farmer with a carrot. We are not forced to live in the farm, but instead choose to. The realizations of Truth behind this human farm that we have been living in for so long can shatter a person's reality and change their life forever. That is why once you fully understand this information and become consciously aware of Truth, you will join the ranks of all of those individuals who proudly proclaim they are "awake". By understanding these fundamental Truths to reality it will be like opening your eyes from what seemed like an endless nightmare. (2, 6, 11)

CHAPTER 4

EXPANDING CONSCIOUSNESS

Stop for a moment and close your eyes. Visualize seeing yourself from the third person, like a silent observer floating above. Now slowly zoom out, further and further, until you pass through the clouds and out of our atmosphere. Continue ascending until you leave Earth and are merely left with a tiny blue speck, quietly revolving through space. Feel for a moment that almost inconceivable wonder and complete humbleness of your very existence right now. This minuscule blue planet, surrounded by the vast darkness of space, is the only home we have ever known. Allow this enhanced perception to flow through the fabric of what defines your existence. By using this model of awareness as a grounding point for the expansion of consciousness, all distractions that seek to derail our enhancement simply vanish into thin air, exposing themselves for the illusions that they really are.

The idea that we are on a planet right now flying through space isn't something most people think about. It's almost as if we forget where we really are and collectively pretend to be on the set of an egotistical reality show. That false perception is what feeds the created reality which still firmly grips society. I often find myself standing at the crossroads of a busy intersection, observing people as they quickly rush past one another and ponder who they each are and where they are going. I think about what this illusion of our reality has done to each and every one of them. From the lonely elderly woman heading home to eat a microwave dinner by herself to the corporate businessman locked away in an upscale office, wondering when he will get home to his family, all I see here is sadness. I see this tremendous sadness from the lack of connection to our external world and most importantly to ourselves.

Humanity has been made to believe that our individual contributions and consequences aren't real and that every action is random and meaningless. This delusion to our existence is simply based on nothing. Yet this perception has poisoned our minds and closed us off from any experience that doesn't bring instant pleasure. What kind of a life would each person decide to live if only they knew the Truths of their existence? Would they really settle for these mundane and shallow activities that fill up this physical life here? As the clock for our own mortality ticks away, we must ask ourselves if this is the life we really wanted to live.

By repositioning our mind to strongly consider the feelings of every human being and stripping away the segregation of race that is so ingrained into our psyche, the expansion of consciousness can occur quite rapidly. The great secret that has been kept from humanity is what accompanies our unique emotion. Human emotion allows connection to the higher self and is intrinsically important for the evolution of consciousness. If the individual does not connect to their emotional side, the ancient left brain dominates their perception of reality and fundamentally changes how they even identify with themselves. Without emotion, we become locked in a red frequency state and disconnected to consciousness.

With all of the negative associations mocking emotion in our society, the most important trait that makes us human has almost been forgotten to us. By reconnecting to our true emotional side and allowing our heart to govern our actions, the path towards enlightenment welcomes us with loving arms. It doesn't matter what has happened in the past because the mistakes we have made do not control the future. The only thing that really matters is the moment you are in right now. Instead of using sight as the primary means for direction, try following the ancient guidance found within intuition itself. By following this inner voice of intuition, the road towards the expansion of consciousness and self-discovery unfolds within us like a divine river of progression.

The most difficult obstacle in the expansion of consciousness, and breaking free of this illusion of our mind is actually our self. As a society, we have been programmed to distrust new information and push away anything that challenges the simple narrative that governs our lives. These "blocks" inside of us maintain the status of who we think we are and the comfortability in this reality. When new information comes along that challenges everything in a person's paradigm, the natural response is to push that negative feeling away and try to remain in a state of blissful ignorance. That perfectly normal reaction is the main blocking mechanism for new information being understood and absorbed.

The human subconscious has been trained to attack any new ideas that disrupt the designated reality chosen for society. Discovering the Truths within all of this and expanding consciousness, was never meant to be easy. Held back at almost every turn, the remarkable story of humanity and its place in the universe is really just beginning. What an indescribable feeling it is to know that we are not alone and that humans are part of something incredible. The secret gifts found within humanity are ultimately the reason for so much of our suppression. Once society is able to collectively shed the controlled manipulation of reality, we will finally step out from the shackles that limited our awareness, to see a world filled with infinite possibilities and the fundamentally important experiences that lead to our own conscious expansion.

The best analogy for describing humanity's control of consciousness, and the state of fear that has stagnated our expansion for so long is through the Allegory of the Cave metaphor. This clever analogy by Plato perfectly illustrates the means by which our society has been kept locked in a cave of its own awareness. The Allegory of the Cave categorizes where each person would fall relative to their level of conscious awareness of information and Truth. In this dark cave, there are captors and captives. The captives represent the majority of humanity, who are chained to a fixed position which only allows them to stare at one spot on the cave wall. Behind them are the captors, who use fire to project shadows on the wall in front of the captives. The captives are unaware of their captors because they exist in a smaller box of awareness then them. The captors use these shadows as tools for fear to control the chained population who is convinced that the shadows are real. What most of the captives do not know is that they are actually not a prisoner from anything but themselves. The chains that bind them and fears that control their expansion are simply a clever illusion to distract them from the Truth. The last group of people represents the freed prisoners, who are no longer bounded by the cave, or false shadows that keep them enchained. These free thinkers exist outside the cave, far from darkness and are illuminated by the light of Truth.

Once a person becomes free of all these illusions, they must then decide if they are going to return to the cave to try and help the other prisoners, or simply exist in their own state of bliss above ground, in the warmth of the light. This important decision is the ultimate deciding factor for the outcome of humanity. As a collective community, we must search ourselves for the compassion that exists within, to care about the welfare of our fellow humans. This struggle is all of ours to bear and only together will we decide if it is worth fighting for.

In realizing our own misunderstood identity, we must first come to terms with understanding the importance of the chakra system in the body. The chakra system represents activation points for important DNA as we continuously evolve our consciousness. Isn't it incredible to learn that there are seven colors to the visible light spectrum as well as seven chakras in the human body? What is even more amazing is that these seven chakras centers directly relate to the matching wavelengths of visible light. Does that mean we are really light beings with amnesia?

The most important thing to understand and ultimate key to our evolution, lies in what we are on the smallest level. The information being taught in school for describing the core functionality behind vibration and frequency within the human body is almost non-existent and cleverly omitted. The foundation for the expansion of consciousness is built on the understanding of these intrinsically important aspects of human mentality. All species on Earth are composed of atoms that are in various states of vibration and frequency. Even the planet we call home has its own unique vibratory rate and sound if recorded from space. Every action and reaction of matter is defined by the specific frequency it exists within. All information is received optimally within human beings in a higher state of vibration. This chapter is intended for assisting the expansion of your consciousness and freeing your mind, through raising your vibration and frequency.

If the majority of the population exists in a state of low vibration and frequency, then the direct result will be a society functioning within a collectedly shared awareness. Each individual person affects the energy field and frequency of those around them and that becomes compounded exponentially through population density in larger communities. Envision a group of friends sitting outside under the sun on a blue sky day, full of laughter and happiness together. Because the group is collectively choosing to remain in a positive state of frequency, a flow of energy is connected between them, lifting their moods to a higher state. Suddenly one of the friends receives a phone call informing them that a loved one has been tragically killed and they begin to cry. Instantly the feeling changes between the group as something has darkened or altered the atmosphere. What has happened is that the frequency rate from the result of sadness, fear, or hate, has brought the collective groups down to their level. This is of course, is not the fault of the person grieving, but rather the emotional acceptance of slower frequency through our intense need for human compassion for others.

Along with the importance of understanding frequency and vibration, the next step in the process of expanding consciousness is achieved through unlocking the secret and highly guarded third eye for the brain, known as the pineal gland. When functioning correctly this special gland connects our forgotten antenna, providing fundamental insight and expanding our perception and awareness of reality. The pineal gland has throughout history been called the third eye because it allows a way to see the Truth and break free of the stubborn associations that enslave us. This gland can be activated through raising the bodies functioning vibratory rate and consciously seeking expansion of the mind. Because of the accumulations of Fluoride and other toxins in the body, this gland remains blocked and dormant inside of us. To be successful in expanding your consciousness, you must reconnect with this ancient center of knowledge. The way of activating the human pineal gland is found through meditation, optimal health, and the use of certain plant allies found on Earth.

All of the tainted foods and water mentioned in the suppression chapter are ultimately designed to lower our vibration and block off the expansion provided by the pineal gland so that we ultimately exist in a red spectrum of ourselves. Years of accumulated neurotoxins in the body cause the pineal gland to become crystallized and dormant. One of the most important things a person can do to expand their consciousness is by eating healthy, organic foods and drinking natural spring water.

The reason sudden expansions or awakenings can occur in an individual in rapid time is directly related to the activation and cleansing of this intrinsically important gland. Ancient cultures revered this third eye and its deep purpose to us as a species. The importance of the pineal gland for conscious expansion has been worshiped and engraved into many of the most famous landmarks from our distant past. The pineal gland is most notably seen in ancient Egyptian culture and is shown frequently as the eye of Ra, or eye of Horus. By discovering this Truth within ourselves, we are able to connect with the very source of knowledge itself and rapidly transition to a new state of conscious awareness.

After thousands of years of accumulated war, greed, and fear, much of humanity has become locked in a stagnant state of its own false illusion. Peppered throughout the masses are those who exist in a high vibration and challenge the very nature of everything. Those gifted individuals who have a high state of vibration are able to raise the vibration of others around them and actually alter their reality. Like beacons of light in stormy, dark waters, they constantly battle to hold their vibration up and remain positive. A good example can be seen with the transition of someone lonely and sad into falling in love. Since our emotions connect us with a higher vibration, the answer for finding true happiness lies within love and compassion. It does not have to be love for a person, but love as the means for every decision and action taken. By deciding to embrace love for others and most importantly yourself, the expansion of consciousness into a more peaceful state of growth can occur quickly for those who are completely free of fear and hate. By releasing all fear and hate inside, we become the state we were meant to exist in all along.

There are a lot of ways to expand consciousness, and each

individual has their own methods that work for them based on their body type and neural functions. For example, some individuals do not like the effects of psychedelics and prefer a completely natural approach. We each have our own unique methods that provide assistance and only through self-discovery can those be found. Meditation is essential for those who want to truly expand their consciousness. Meditation provides a deep reflecting point for the soul, through clearing the mind of distractions and helping to connect to your multidimensional side. When a person goes into a deep meditative state, they are able to seek balance, as well as receive important insight for those who can listen.

Meditation has been falsely viewed by the majority of society as a sort of myth, or alternative science for the body. Meditation is essential for achieving balance and happiness and could alleviate the suffering for millions of people around the world. Even those individuals who do not have the intention of expanding their consciousness will find great peace and balance in this practice.

What meditation does that is so intrinsically important is that it slows down and clears the mind of pollution, to bring the body to a state of complete mind over matter. All of the thoughts controlling and determining every action we make are melted away in a state of serenity until all that remains is the moment you are in. If an individual practices this yogi lifestyle long enough, everything in their life will change. Once a person fully understands the state of being completely in the moment and seeking balance from within, all of the rest will simply fall into place naturally.

The path of expanding consciousness through the use of meditation takes practice to master and isn't supposed to come easily. I recommend finding a solitary, quiet location, with no distractions from the outside world. Find an appropriate style of music that allows a deep, quiet connection to the self. Start by sitting cross-legged on the floor and closing your eyes. Breathe in deeply, holding your breath for a few moments and then slowly exhale. Repeat this over and over, until you naturally fall into a rhythm of your own breathing. Feel the energy flowing through your body and clear your mind of all thought. Do not try and force anything or become frustrated with a lack of progress. Instead, just exist in a state of complete peace and quiet. Remind yourself that you are not defined by your physical body and that you exist as only your pure consciousness on another dimensional plane. Just when you are about to give up and stop trying is the moment you will truly feel the deep connection to your higher self and realize you are meditating.

When in a higher meditative state, great wisdom is often given through visions and thoughts to those who are listening. This important state of mind is the lost connection we have forgotten to ourselves. So much of humanity constantly suffers from feeling alone in this existence, unaware that there is a place they could go to take away all of that pain and find peace and purpose within themselves. The art of meditation goes back for thousands of years and is one of the greatest secrets kept from us. Think of the seemingly lonely monk, choosing to devote their life to the idea of protecting something deeper and intrinsically important to all of humanity. But what is so important that an individual gives up all material things for? The meditative state provides a critical connection back to all life in the universe and the important role for where human beings fit in. Through tearing down the false veil of reality provided to us, meditation exposes the true heart of our divine purpose.

One of the most essential means for the expansion of consciousness is found through the lost connections back to Gaia itself. The incredible beauty found on planet Earth has all but been forgotten by most of society, driven by the illusions of material wealth and the manipulation of reality. By reconnecting with the heart of Gaia herself, an important piece of our expansion and identity can finally be found. The connections and quiet found within nature, free of all distractions, provides the greatest lessons we could possibly learn about ourselves. There is great wisdom to be gained through spending time with Mother Nature and listening to the subtle whispers from a gently flowing stream or the somber creak and sway of an ancient old growth tree. These connections back to the Earth provide the very means for our conscious evolution.

The important connections back to Gaia and quiet itself, has been replaced in society by the distracting screams from all of the electronic devices that we identify ourselves with. Even in my short lifetime, I have seen a complete disappearance of the importance of growing up and playing in the outdoors. Society has replaced the external world with the illusion of its technological accomplishments. Technology can be a powerful tool for expansion, but far more commonly it becomes the substitute for vital exercise and fresh air, turning us into a society of confused, caged animals. We have forgotten our important connection to the natural world and the need for peace and quiet that it provides us. Slowly eroded from within us through years of conditioning and conformity, most people today just avoid nature and the quiet completely.

With so much stacked against human conscious expansion from the many pollutants that contaminate our minds, we must look to nature in order to provide a safe haven back to reality. One of the greatest unsung heroes for the conscious expansion of humanity is found within the natural plant psychedelics found on Earth. This special group of plants and fungi alter human consciousness and free the bonds of linear thinking while raising vibration and frequency. So much of our conscious expansion can be linked back to their use that our very evolution as a species may not have happened without them. All throughout history, ancient cultures have revered these sacred allies for teaching and wisdom. The most crucial lesson that humanity can learn from the guidance given from these plants, is the importance of reconnecting the left and right brains and finally finding balance within.

For the individual considering any psychedelic, it must be done with respect and in the correct setting. These ancient plants and fungi are very powerful and can change the very fabric of reality itself. The reason the setting is so critical for their use is that the experience can dramatically change depending on the individual. Since these plant healers have been deliberately demonized for so many generations, a strong stigma still looms over their use in society. Before you ever decide to try one, do extensive and objective research to learn everything about their properties and how they interact with the human body. The degree of benefit found from these plants will vary greatly amongst individuals. For some people, they will find enormous healing and knowledge, while in others, anxiety, and unpleasantness. Every human functions within their own unique level and must seek out that which provides the greatest assistance to their own advancement. Even these important healers themselves must be used with balance and respect in order to achieve success with them.

The expansion of consciousness is the greatest achievement an individual can do for their personal growth as a developing species on this planet. The road to expanding consciousness is like being lost in a dark forest with no map to follow. Countless pathways lead to dead ends, forcing us to come back to where we started over and over again. The only way to find the correct path towards the light of Truth is by following the breadcrumbs laid down by like-minded individuals and connecting to our deep spiritual side. In this physical plane of reality that we stumble through in an attempt to discover our deep purpose within life itself, our path towards expansion follows the great narrative being played out all around us for the very evolution of the universe itself.

CHAPTER 5

THE EVOLUTION OF CONSCIOUSNESS

What is an idea and where does it come from? Throughout human history, an intellectual breakthrough will often occur with a unique individual, whose effects will ripple out and change the very fabric of our comprehension for what is possible. These brilliant minds, like Newton or Einstein, provided tremendous leaps forward for us as a species. These great breakthroughs rapidly change the stagnant momentum of the public and rewrite history. It only takes a small handful of these gifted individuals among billions of people on planet Earth, to ultimately be responsible for leading all of society forward. With every new generation comes the inherent ability for an expanded awareness of the outside world, and an increased acceptance of all of humanity itself, regardless of race. Building upon this increased awareness and acceptance, these important social values will be handed down to the next generation of children, who truly represent the key to the future during this sweeping revolution of conscious change.

But are we really coming up with these integral ideas merely on our own? We must return to the original question at hand and examine where an idea really comes from. If we are merely organic bodies that house our true energy within consciousness, then we must separate random synapses in the brain for being the only source of new ideas. Since human beings are mostly water based, and function off of electrical currents which utilize various frequencies, then we must reevaluate our unique identity and stop allowing ourselves to become distracted by that which means to disconnect us.

If you were to try and define the human species and the potentials available in an enlightened state, it would resemble an energetic antenna for tremendous information which can create powerful mental abilities. As we become more aware and healthier, our vibration rises, along with our capacity for information to be received. This multistep process of expanding consciousness and having the ability of receiving high amounts of information is what drives our evolution as a species. But what information are we tapping into and how could that even be possible? These are the questions we must ask in the search for true answers.

Light is the transmitter of all information and provider for most of life in the universe. The primary creators of light are suns found within each solar system. When I refer to an interconnected universe and one which follows a precise mathematical formula in its incredible design, I speak of a plan which seeks to become aware all along. Found hidden inside our brains with the activation of the pineal gland, humans are able to connect to this ancient knowledge center of Truth, calling to us with increasing intensity as we continue to accelerate our own evolution. These records which propel our own expansion have been called the Akashic records and have been spoken about by ancient spiritual cultures for thousands of years. This Truth we seek is not found through chaos, but in uniform lessons and ideas, all feeding to the same outcome. We must simply step outside and feel the warmth of the sun's rays and allow them to peel away the veil which holds back our conscious expansion.

The most incredible part in this entire story of us, are those who seek to hold back our awareness and evolution, while at the same time, being countered by humanities increasing need for expansion. This battle of light over darkness has been occurring in the universe for millions of years. We are nearing the conclusion of that long fought battle now, when the children of the Source itself rise up and take back what has been their purpose all along. Humanity holds within itself the divine spark which propels everything in the universe. All of the violence and submission of our free will, has been an attempt to extinguish this sacred spark all along. The agenda for millennia has been to block us from remembering our true identity and remain asleep for all of time. What hope would we have here, seemingly alone, put up against such insurmountable odds? That hidden identity to humanity is why so much has been sacrificed here on this planet and held back from us discovering. This entire Illusion of Us all stems from the original jealously over who we really are and the severe objection from the fallen Lucifer and his loyal angels. We must decipher if these are merely just stories, or teachings aimed at conveying the design for duality itself. Once we wake up to this injustice of our consciousness, we will finally be able take back our own future.

There is no questioning the fact that humanity has been enslaved and held back for thousands of years, with the illusion of a false identity controlling our every action. The most fascinating aspect of this for me is the notion that our own expedited evolution is perhaps being assisted from those who believe in the survival and freedom of the human race. There are many advanced cultures from all over the stars that couldn't bear to simply stand by and helplessly watch the enslavement of the human race. These original planners of the living library on Earth represented the ancient alliances which protected the uninterrupted development of the human species. These were the forgotten guardians of this planet and those who fight for the preservation of free will and Truth in the universe. These peaceful interstellar races are greatly interested in the outcome of humanity and the breaking free of enslavement from those who bind us. When you begin to realize the monumental scope of everything happening around our planet it begins to sound very similar to the premise of a Star Wars movie. Perhaps that is the point all along.

Hidden inside cleverly designed movies, games, and books, these similarities speak to those who are consciously aware and looking for answers. We must draw connections for where the inspiration for so many of these "science fiction" ideas derived from originally. The underlying message is that most elaborate stories and those with hidden symbology are almost always based on something real. When you start looking for these connections or repetitive themes, you realize that they are everywhere all around us. All that stands in the way of this discovery for most people is the disbelief within themselves that anything can be connected. Once this false illusion is removed, nothing will stand in the way of conscious expansion.

The number one reason why humanity as a whole has not connected to its deeper spiritual side, which follows these important correlated symbols, is due to our own ego blocking us off. Of all the human traits which cause us such a disconnection from ourselves, ego is by far the most destructive. What ego does that is so dangerous to the expansion of humanity, is that it manifests the false idea of our greatness simply based on what our minor achievements have been in the past. This measurement of our identity based on our accomplishments, which is widely promoted through material possession and the worship of idols, has forced society to lose almost all sense of true self. These distractions bombard us from every direction and seek to have us finally forget, once and for all.

The hidden symbols that surround us all the time, separate out the Truth and what is actually real, with what has been created in our mind as an illusion to distract us. By reconnecting with planet Earth and deciphering the meanings behind these ancient teachings, we will suddenly understand so much of what has been hiding in plain sight all along. The many advanced races who wish to see the growth of our consciousness use these symbols and hidden messages as a means of communicating important ideas that can propel us forward at critical junctions.

Even consciousness itself, from within a human being, cannot be necessarily limited to just the origins of Earth. We must strongly consider the idea that certain people here are literally extraterrestrial consciousness, sent back from another time in order to make a difference. These unique people are assumed by the masses to just be human, even though deep down inside they have always known a Truth that was bubbling just below the surface. That truth is the fact that consciousness is far from limited to only the human species. So much of the future of Earth could come down to a mere handful of these dedicated and passionate souls. The outcome of humanity on Earth may have a profound rippling effect on the entire universe itself.

Here we are, at this critical juncture in human evolution, teetering on the very brink of our own mutual destruction, and racing towards a future which lies within our own immature, shaky hands. Within a population of over 7 billion people on the planet, there are millions who are waking up to these Truths of our life. This explosion of our conscious expansion is largely due to the availability of connecting with like-minded individuals and reliable sources of information. The stunning thing about this transformation is that most of this information is coming from the collective of humanity itself. As we share knowledge across every corner of our globe, we have become a connected online society and are breaking free of all forms of suppression. Each person then empowers themselves to become an influential tool for spreading information. As this information spreads out and more people continue to wake up to the Truths of their existence here, they begin to see through the lies and manipulation that bombard us constantly. Awakened people start to block these distractions out of their lives and take the reins of their own destiny. These individuals reexamine everything in their life and often make dramatic, life altering decisions based on this new found sense of direction.

The beautiful thing about this life we are living is how we can change so profoundly and quickly with the right environment and encouragement. Nothing that happens in our past should ever discourage what can be in the future. The only thing that dictates future events is the moment you are in right now. Once we make the crucial decision inside our mind to change, it can take what seems like only a moment to begin down the right path. That path is something all of us should consciously decide to take, for it leads to the very expansion of everything in our life. By absorbing stimulating information that challenges our mind, we push the limits of our own comprehension. By arriving at this state of total amazement over a new idea never pondered before, the brain breaks free of the chains of its previous limitations to its own awareness. The secret behind conscious expansion is in the very word expansion itself. By enlarging the perspective for the world around us, it forces our conscious evolution. That is all evolution is at its heart, the physical or mental growth of a species which enhances it. We must stop looking at evolution through the lens of simply physical attributes. Whereas physical evolution may take millions of years, conscious evolution can occur dramatically in a very short period of time.

Ignorance may seem like bliss to many people right now, but that is only because it is one of the last safe refuges for our emotions. By ignoring that which instills fear and pulls down happiness, it can be a temporary island of peace. But this island is not meant to stay on forever, for if too many decide to live there, our future will simply sink away from all around us. Ignorance creates a world where humanity wears a permanent blindfold to the horrible atrocities eating away at our very freedoms and destroying our home. By the time we decide we are ready to remove these blindfolds and see the Truth, it may already be too late. We must learn to balance our intake of Truthful information, verse knowing when to block out that which takes from our well-being and drains our emotional side.

Conscious expansion forms new ideas in the brain through passion and excitement, allowing the connected neurons to fuse together inside, until all of a sudden you realize you understand yet another piece of the puzzle. If we are able to move beyond the decisions we have made in the past without guilt, we can realize that all that is left to life is experience and learning. All of the careless mistakes we have made, successes we have achieved, or relationships we have formed, all play a key part of our story and the experience we are having.

The world has been perceived to us as a hostile and barbaric place, largely by the influences of the mainstream media. As we have increased our access to technology and social media, we have begun to see the cracks in these lies. So many have simply canceled their cable subscriptions and found much more happiness once again because of it. Their lives are no longer dominated by fear and hate and instead project a much different reality. Over time more and more have realized this and have found a deep happiness they never knew existed.

Humanity has become a global community that is more connected than at any other time in our history. All of the great minds and sacrifices made by so many brave individuals contribute to the overall narrative of humanity. Carl Sagan eloquently said,

"Look again at that blue dot. That's here. That's home. That's us. On it everyone you love, everyone you know, everyone you ever heard of, every human being who ever was, lived out their lives. The aggregate of our joy and suffering, thousands of confident religions, ideologies, and economic doctrines, every hunter and forager, every hero and coward, every creator and destroyer of civilization, every king and peasant, every young couple in love, every mother and father, hopeful child, inventor and explorer, every teacher of morals, every corrupt politician, every 'superstar,' every 'supreme leader,' every saint and sinner in the history of our species lived there-on a mote of dust suspended in a sunbeam." Carl Sagan not only expanded our awareness of space, but he was able to even alter our perceptions of ourselves as well. The contributions to our conscious expansion made by Sagan and so many other gifted minds will echo in eternity for their essential role in our own success.

The precise design woven into the progression and evolution of humanity is simply beautiful and humbling to observe if you are able to see how all the pieces fit together. The global collective is quickly realizing the illusions behind fear and the essential need for dismantling the military-industrial complex. Humans are now traveling to most of the countries on Earth for either business or leisure and spreading their perspectives and knowledge to all parts of society. This cultural infusion of ideas, compounded by the expansions brought on by the internet, has led to the runaway conscious awakening for all of humanity. The notable exceptions for this interconnected society lie within countries like North Korea, Iraq, and Syria, where a perpetual cycle of warfare or tyranny, has plagued the poor people of the region for decades. These countries are then portrayed in the spotlight of the media in order to show instability and create fear, to instill the illusion of a dangerous world.

The darker ways of the past are crumbling all around us as society yearns to satisfy its increasing desire for peace and love building within. No longer will humanity accept this enslavement through fear, instigated through perpetual warfare that has gripped us for so long. This profound change can be clearly seen in the dramatic transformation of politics around the world. This global revolution has swept through countless dictators and monarchies, like an enormous tidal wave of conscious change for all of humanity. The old forms of government which have controlled society for so long through the use of tyranny and fear are quickly being replaced by those who seek peace, compassion, and feel a responsibility in protecting the future.

A fascinating aspect of this global revolution of consciousness to consider are the fundamental changes within humanity which have directly led to this intriguing outcome. The best metaphor for describing our current state of expansion is from the vantage point of a simmering pot of water on a hot stove. The pot represents the control and suppression of human conscious expansion, with the simmering water inside that of society. No matter how tight the lid is held on the pot, eventually the water will boil over and spill everywhere. The underlying Truth is that the water inside the pot was never meant to be contained in the first place. This spilling out, or revolution of Truth, encapsulates every human being on the planet. Driven by our increasingly connected world, the collective of humanity itself is speeding towards a profound awakening. Moving at almost light speed, so much is changing so fast, that many of the leaders of the old guard are left simply scratching their heads in confusion.

The Earth is still considered a Class 0 planet, according to the brilliant professor Michio Kaku, and it isn't hard to see when looking at our culture from the point of an objective observer. We still have a long way to go before we can claim the title of a peaceful Class 1 planet. The biggest challenge for the human species will be realizing the need to protect the planet we call home for a future that can sustain us. By reconnecting with Gaia, the embodiment of our planet, a strong relationship can be made with the Earth to allow us to remember what we have forgotten so long ago. The wise ancients of the past knew how intrinsically important this connection was to the growth of the soul. Instead of looking purely outward to propel humanity's expansion, we must first start by looking right under our feet. By understanding this planet and our purpose here, we can begin to move away from the dark days of the past and instead look only towards the future.

There is no escaping this evolution of humanity, for it is written into the framework of the cosmos itself. Prophesized by the Mayans thousands of years ago, this new age is a period when darkness no longer rules this planet and balance will seek itself out in every ray of cosmic light that spreads across this vast universe. All of life itself is merely the dream of endless creation and death coming to a dramatic and beautiful conclusion. There is nothing to fear with death as it is always followed by rebirth. The true human identity is not found by looking externally at the physical body but through the perspective of energy and consciousness. Our multidimensional consciousness is what ultimately defines our existence here. It is who we really are on the deepest level and by using this physical body, we are able to experience a three-dimensional world. When we die, we are reborn into a new body to learn from the mistakes of the past. Fear, stemming from the lack of our own identity, is the clever illusion that has bound us for so long. In redefining the human species, we must crack open the walls of Darwin's cave in order to finally see the Truth in our self.

Every day that we open our eyes, there is a new chance at infinite possibilities to occur. There is a wave of conscious change that has swept across the globe awakening the masses. It can be felt in the changing perspectives of how we define ourselves, even if we aren't aware of it at the time. This advancement of all technology, influencing every part of our society, has finally formed a global collective consciousness. This giant leap forward has been propelled by the invention of the internet, followed by social media on nearly every portable device. Suddenly we have all become interconnected and are able to interact with other people anywhere in the world. It became a global consciousness aware of itself and evolving from within. Like the butterfly effect, our very actions have led to an alternate reality, where we are choosing peace over prescribed war. Without these technological advancements, none of us would still be here.

To understand this conscious evolution from the perspective of modern science, quantum physics, and specifically string theory, give us a glimpse into the incredible mechanics behind this finite universe. They show the intricate designs behind this holographic universe, made up of almost infinite strings of information vibrating at various frequencies. All matter is determined by its unique vibrational structure. This gets to the very core of the duality of the universe itself. This fluctuation of vibration and frequency is what drives all evolution. The laws of nature following a complex code which design the stage for all of matter. A finely tuned universe so precise, that a simple fraction of a difference and none of it would have existed at all. These are the telltale signs left behind of a forgotten master architect, expressing itself in the grand theater of life. William Shakespeare once brilliantly wrote, "All the world's a stage, and all the men and women merely players; they have their exits and their entrances; and one man in his time plays many parts, his acts being seven ages."

This coming of the Golden Age in our solar system, or awakening, is the accelerated evolution of humanity. This awakening simply can't be delayed any longer, as society on Earth transitions into the Age of Aquarius. The more this human collective is held back, the larger the leaps are down the line. This river of expansion with its countless dams at every turn refuses to slow down, for its momentum has been written into the story of the river itself all along. William Blake once wrote, "If the doors of perception were cleansed, everything would appear to man as it is, infinite."

When looking at human progression and the appalling means for which our growth has been delayed, the inevitable conclusion may seem simple on the surface, until you peel back the cleverly hidden teachings of duality that rule the universe. The cumulative aftermath of the slumbering of consciousness in humanity for so long will ultimately lead its own evolution on a monumentally fast level. When one starts to understand the connections of everything in the universe and the intimate role that every living creature plays, they realize that for this duality to truly work there must also exist a darker side which is able to counter the light and bring harmony to a perfect system of growth. If evil didn't exist there would be no lessons to define what good really is. Everything is happening precisely as it should, at the exact moment it needs to.

We must understand that because of the darkness, there can be light. This is what duality represents at its heart and core in the never-ending search for balance, hidden within the mirage of chaos. If humanity is able to sincerely learn from the mistakes of their past, there will be nothing stopping their infinite future. This solution is found hidden amidst the delicate dance between the two pieces of the same energy which combine to make up the whole.

It is at that moment when you realize the answers have been staring at us in the face all along, found in common symbols like the Yin Yang, that have been patiently waiting for the right time when they can be understood. The divine gifts that the human species have are finally being revealed as we wipe away the grogginess of our misunderstood identity. We are the windows that perceive the universe itself and record its story for all of time.

From every tragedy to the most beautiful moments of love and humble amazement, every unique experience we have directly leads back to the Source of all life itself. We are all playing an important part in shaping the very story of humanity. Know that anytime you feel lonely or lost, there is always compassionate wisdom to be found by searching within and discovering your own divine Truths. Like tiny fragments of light flickering in a sea of darkness, it only takes a small amount of courage to truly see. (1, 8)

Bibliography

1) Marciniak, Barbara, "Bringers of the Dawn: Teachings from the Pleiadians", Bear and Company, 1992, Rochester.
2) Sitchin, Zecharia, "The 12th Planet", Ishi Press, 1976, New York.
3) Pye, Lloyd, "Everything you Know is Wrong, Book One: Human Origins", iUniverse, 2000.
4) Plato, "Timaeus and Critias", Pantianos Classics, 1871, England.
5) Clark, Gerald R., "The 7th Planet Mercury Rising", Create Space Self-Publishing, 2013.
6) Doreal, "The Emerald Tablets of Thoth the Atlantean", Source Books, 1930, Gallatin, TN.
7) Dalley, Stephanie, "Myths from Mesopotamia: Creation, the Flood, Gilgamesh, and others", 2000, Kensington Oxford University Press, Oxford.
8) Temple, Robert, "The Sirius Mystery", Destiny Books, 1998, Rochester, VT

Credits

Barbara Marciniak (1), David Icke (2), Graham Hancock (3), Randall Carlson (4), Robert Temple (5), Dr Steven Greer (6), Zecharia Sitchin (7), Michio Kaku (8), Michael Tellinger (9), Robert Bauval (10), Dr. John Brandenburg (11), William Cooper (12), Michael Dues and Mary Brown (13), Mark Passio (14), Gerald Clark (15)

ABOUT THE AUTHOR

Matthew LaCroix is a passionate writer and researcher who grew up in the outdoors of northern New England. From an early age, a strong connection back to nature was established and built into the morals of his life. His persistent yearning for adventure led him into profound, life-changing experiences that inspired him to write for local and national magazines such as Backpacker and AMC Outdoors.

While attending Plymouth State University, he published his first book at the age of 22 and began studying history, philosophy, and string theory where his focus became uncovering and connecting the esoteric teachings of the ancient past. At 32 he published his second book entitled; "The Illusion of Us", which combined years of research in the pursuit of truth, ancient history, and understanding the framework to reality.

Made in the USA
Middletown, DE
03 April 2019